AF675081

Olympiad ACE

A Comprehensive Practice Book

for School Olympiads & Talent Search Exams

REASONING

Class 2

BLOOM

Olympiad ACE

A Comprehensive Practice Book

for School Olympiads & Talent Search Exams

REASONING

Class 2

by

Ruchika

Olympiad ACE

BLOOM

Bloom Cap Edu Ventures Pvt. Ltd.

卐 **© Publisher**

No part of this publication may be re-produced, stored in a retrieval system or by any means, electronic, mechanical, photocopying, recording, scanning, web or otherwise without the written permission of the publisher. Publisher has obtained all the information in this book from the sources believed to be reliable and true. However, Publisher or its editors or authors or illustrators don't take any responsibility for the absolute accuracy of any information published and the damage or loss suffered thereupon.

卐 *All disputes subject to Delhi jurisdiction only.*

卐 **Administrative & Production Office**

'Ramchhaya' 4577/15, Agarwal Road, Darya Ganj, New Delhi -110002
Tele: 011- 47630600, 43518550

卐 **PRICE:** ₹125.00

卐 PO No. : TXT-59-T066574-08-25

Published by Arihant Publications (I) Ltd.

For further information about the books log on to
www.bloomcap.org

Follow us on

Preface

"Future belongs to those Who prepares for it today"

School Olympiads are National & International level competitions conducted by different Government, Non-Government & Educational Organisations with the purpose of making the children ready to face competitive exams.

The challenging Questions asked in Olympiads motivate them to learn more & more and bring out the best result with improved academic performance. The Awards & Scholarship offered by Olympiads motivate children to aspire & strive for doing better and emerge out to be the best.

Science Olympiads

Being a Scientist or Engineer or Doctor has always been a dream of each school going child. A good command over Science is a must for any of these. Questions of Science Olympiads are structured to help students to develop scientific temperament & motivate them to understand the concepts of science. They also focuses on improving existing knowledge of a student by adding more information.

'Bloom Science Olympiad Study Book Class 2' is a perfect resource to Study & Practice for Olympiad Exams and other National & State Level Talent Search Exams & Other Competitions.

Some Special Features of Bloom Science Olympiad Study Books are;

- Chapterwise Exercises having different types of Objective Questions; Analytical, Applications, Remembering etc, at par with the Olympiad Level.
- Detailed Explanation for each question.
- Olympiad Pattern Practice Sets at the end.

This book is prepared by Expert Panel with the utmost care, still if you have any suggestions regarding its improvement then feel free to contact us at support@bloomcap.org. We will try to inculcate your suggestions in the further editions.

Contents

01. Matching Pairs 1-4

02. Odd One Out 5-7

03. What Comes Next ? 8-12

04. Coding-Decoding 13-15

05. Complete the Figure 16-20

06. Find Similar Figure and Grouping of Figures 21-25

07. Hidden Figures 26-31

08. Counting of Figures 32-36

09. Position and Comparison Test 37-42

- **Practice Set 1** **45-48**
- **Practice Set 2** **49-55**
- **Hints & Solutions** **56-74**

Chapter 01

Matching Pairs

In 'Matching Pairs', two pairs of figures are given. The figures in first pair are related to each other in some way. In this type of question, students have to find out the missing figure in the second pair. The figures in the second pair are also related in the same way as the figures given in first pair.

EXAMPLE 1 There is a certain relationship between the two figures on the left side of ': :' . Identify the relation and find the missing figure on the right side of ': :' .

(a)  (b)  (c)  (d) 

Sol. *(d)* In first pair, a smiling face appears in the circle, similarly in second pair, a smiling face will appear in the rectangle.

So, figure in option (d) is the missing figure.

Hence, option (d) is correct.

EXAMPLE 2 Choose the number which will complete the second pair.

2 : 4 : : 5 : ?

(a) 7 (b) 8 (c) 3 (d) 9

Sol. *(a)* As, $2+2=4$. In the same way, $5+2=7$

So, number 7 will complete the second pair.

Hence, option (a) is correct.

EXAMPLE 3 Choose the letter which will complete the second pair.

A : C : : ? : G

(a) K (b) L (c) E (d) F

Sol. *(c)* As, A B C = AC, similarly, E F G = EG

So, letter in option (c) will complete the second pair.

Hence, option (c) is correct.

Let's Practice

1. Complete the second pair in the same way as first pair.

(a) (b) (c) (d)

2. Choose the figure which will complete the second pair.

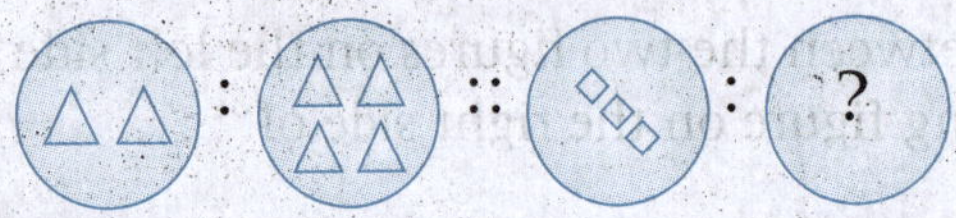

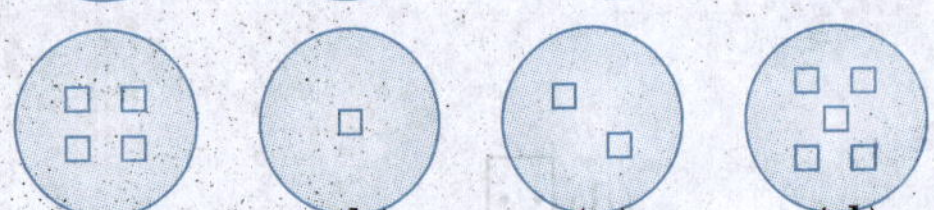

(a) (b) (c) (d)

3. Complete the second pair by choosing a figure from the given alternatives.

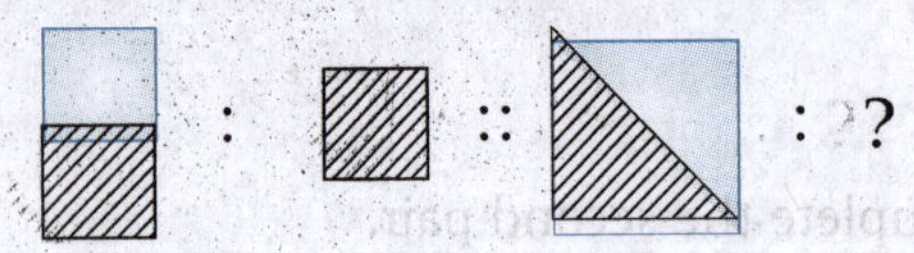

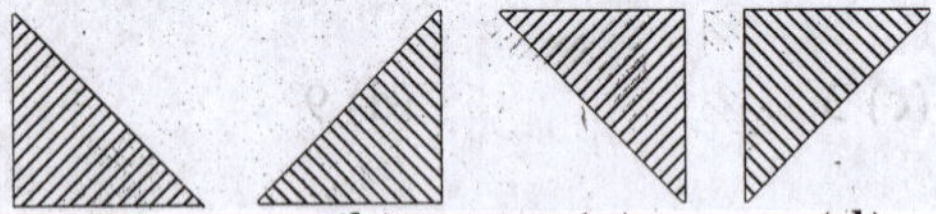

(a) (b) (c) (d)

4. Find the missing figure.

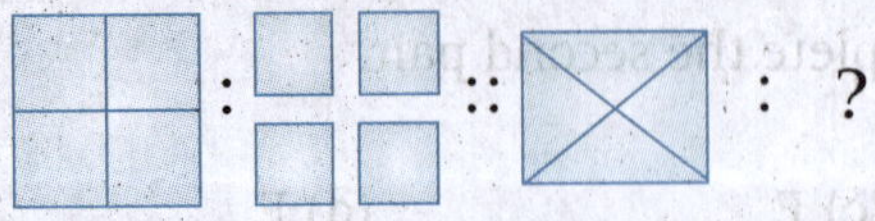

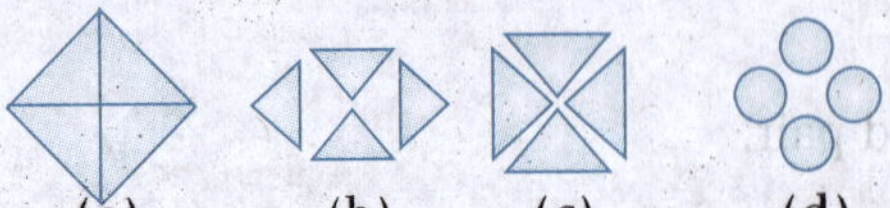

(a) (b) (c) (d)

5. Choose the figure which will complete the second pair.

(a) (b) (c) (d)

6. There is a certain relationship between the figures 1, 3 and 2, 4. Identify the relationship and find the missing figure.

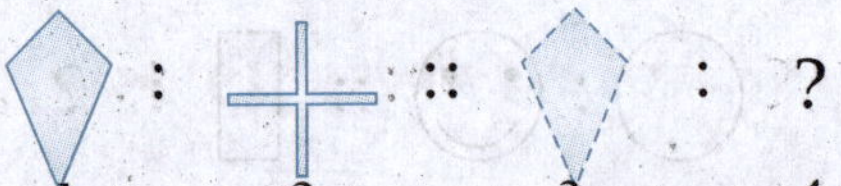

1 2 3 4

(a) (b) (c) (d)

7. Which figure will complete the second pair in the same way as first pair?

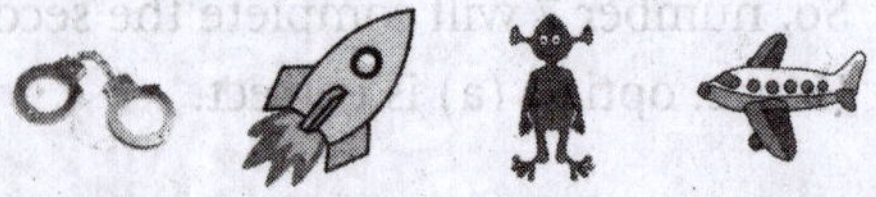

(a) (b) (c) (d)

8. Complete the second pair in the same way as first pair.

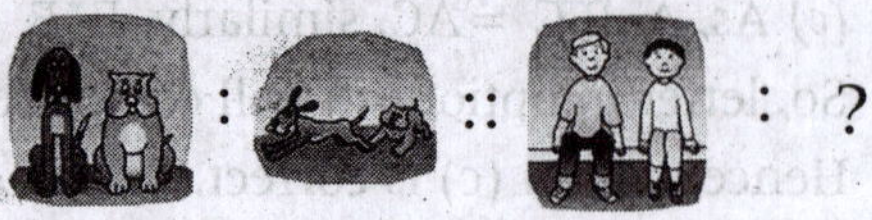

(a) (b) (c) (d)

9. Choose the figure which will complete the second pair.

(a) (b) (c) (d)

10. Complete the second pair in the same way as first pair.

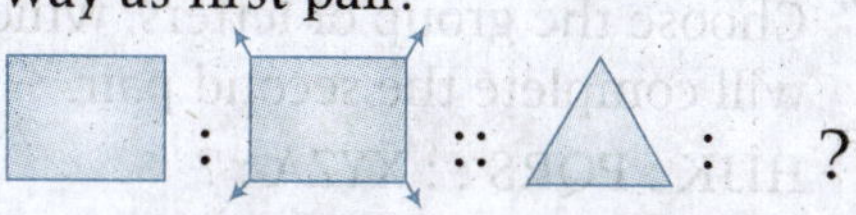

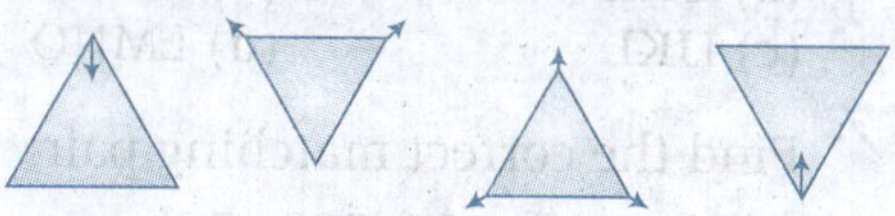

(a) (b) (c) (d)

11. Complete the second pair in the same way as first pair.

(a)  (b) 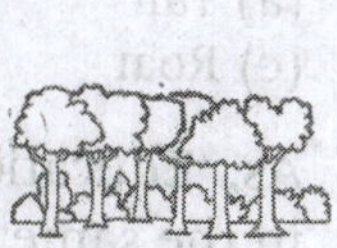

(c)  (d) 

12. Complete the second pair in the same way as first pair.

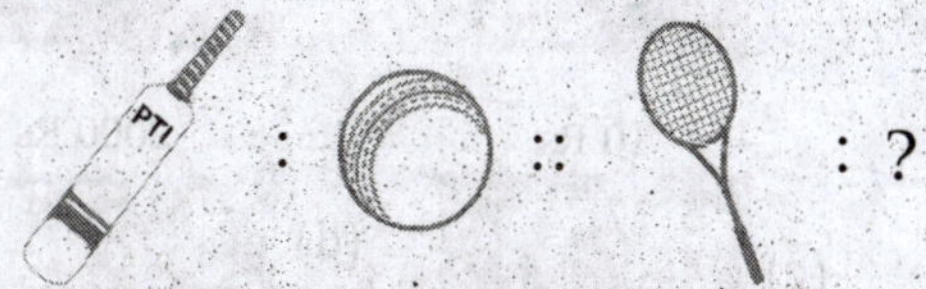

(a) (b) (c) (d)

13. Complete the second pair in the same way as first pair.

(a) (b) (c) (d)

14. Complete the second pair in the same way as first pair.

(a) (b) (c) (d)

15. Complete the second pair in the same way as first pair.

100 Rs 200 Rs 500 Rs

(a) 50 Rs

(b) 1000 Rs

(c) 10 Rs

(d) 2000 Rs

16. Find the missing number.

3 : 7 : : 2 : ?

(a) 8 (b) 7
(c) 6 (d) 9

17. Find the missing number.

18 : 9 : : 17 : ?

(a) 8 (b) 9
(c) 4 (d) 5

18. Which number will complete second pair in the same way as first pair?

2 : 8 : : 5 : ?

(a) 15 (b) 10
(c) 20 (d) 25

19. Find matching pair of second number.

18 : 9 : : 37 : ?

(a) 4 (b) 20
(c) 10 (d) 15

20. Find the number which will complete the second pair.

303 : 405 : : 707 : ?

(a) 404 (b) 908
(c) 808 (d) 809

21. Find the correct matching pair of the following pair.

468 : 797 : : 695 : ?

(a) 9124 (b) 824
(c) 9113 (d) 3119

22. Complete the second pair by choosing a figure from the given alternatives.

J : K : : T : ?

(a) U (b) F
(c) V (d) J

23. Choose the letter which will complete the second pair.

D : G : : I : ?

(a) L (b) M
(c) N (d) P

24. Find the correct matching pair.

Pp : Qq : : Zz : ?

(a) Yy (b) Aa
(c) Uu (d) Xx

25. Find the letter which will complete the second pair.

J : Q : : M : ?

(a) N (b) O
(c) P (d) R

26. Choose the group of letters, which will complete the second pair.

HIJK : PQRS : : XYZA : ?

(a) GHIJ (b) FGHI
(c) IJKL (d) LMNO

27. Find the correct matching pair.

CeGhI : Df : : MoQrS : ?

(a) pN (b) Nm
(c) Nt (d) Np

28. Which word will complete the second pair?

Dog : Bark : : Cat : ?

(a) Tail (b) Mew
(c) Roar (d) Milk

29. As, 'Education' is related to 'School', in the same way 'prayer' is related to?

(a) Church (b) Hospital
(c) Hostel (d) College

30. Which number will complete the second pair ?

MANGO : 25 :: LITCHI : ?

(a) 18 (b) 12
(c) 36 (d) 40

Chapter 02

Odd One Out

'Odd one out' means to find out a figure which is different from all others. In this type of questions, students are given some figures out of which all except one are similar or have some common features. They have to find out the different figure from the given set.

EXAMPLE 1 Find the odd one out.

(a) 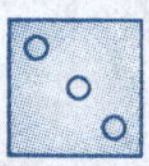 (b) 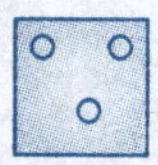 (c) 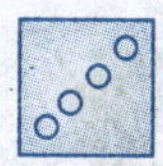 (d) 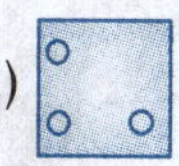

Sol. *(c)* Look at each figure and count the number of circles

(a) 3 circles, (b) 3 circles, (c) 4 circles and (d) 3 circles.

So, except figure (c), all the other figures have same number of circles. Thus, figure (c) is different from others.

Hence, option (c) is correct .

EXAMPLE 2 Four numbers are given below. Choose the one which is different from others.

(a) 6 (b) 8 (c) 5 (d) 4

Sol. *(c)* Except, '5' all others are even numbers. So, option (c) is different from others.

Hence, option (c) is correct.

EXAMPLE 3 Find the odd letter.

(a) BC (b) FG (c) DE (d) BQ

Sol. *(d)* Except, 'BQ' all others are consecutive letters. So, option (d) is different from others.

Hence, option (d) is correct.

EXAMPLE 4 Choose odd one out.

(a) AZ1 (b) MN13 (c) EV7 (d) HS8

Sol. *(c)* Except 'EV7' all others are reverse letter of first letter with English alphabetical position of first letter.

Hence, option (c) is correct.

Let's Practice

1. Which one is different from others?

(a) (b) (c) (d)

2. Choose the figure which is different from others.

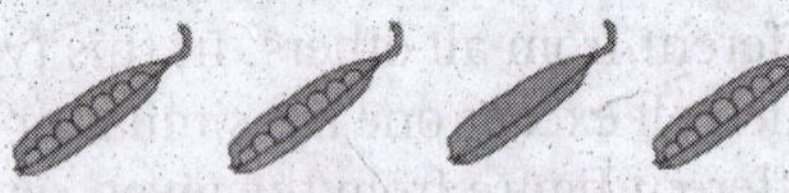

(a) (b) (c) (d)

3. Find the odd one out.

(a) (b) (c) (d)

4. Choose the odd one out.

(a) (b) (c) (d)

5. Find the odd figure.

(a) (b) (c) (d)

6. Choose the odd figure.

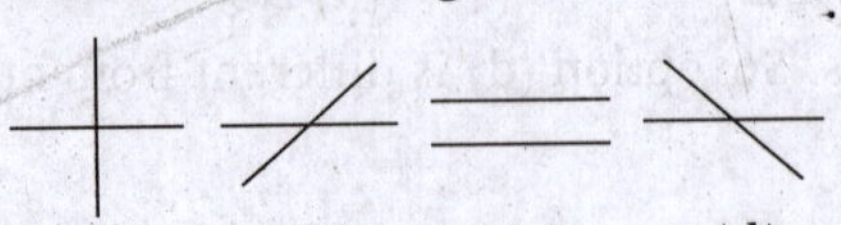

(a) (b) (c) (d)

7. Choose the odd figure.

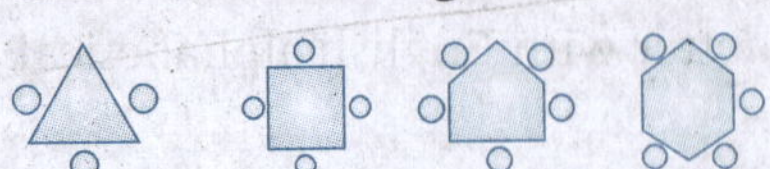

(a) (b) (c) (d)

8. Choose the odd figure.

(a) (b) (c) (d)

9. Find the odd figure.

(a) (b) (c) (d)

10. Choose the figure which is different from others.

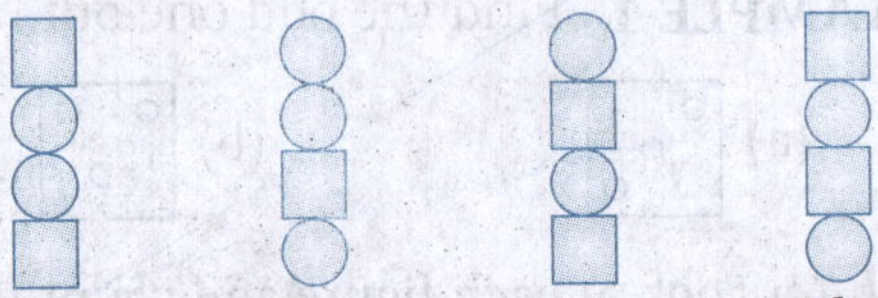

(a) (b) (c) (d)

11. Which one is different from others?

(a) (b) (c) (d)

12. Choose the figure which is different from others?

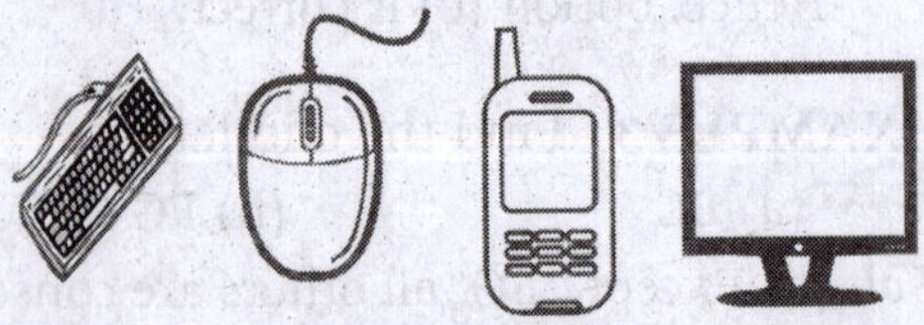

(a) (b) (c) (d)

13. Choose odd one out.

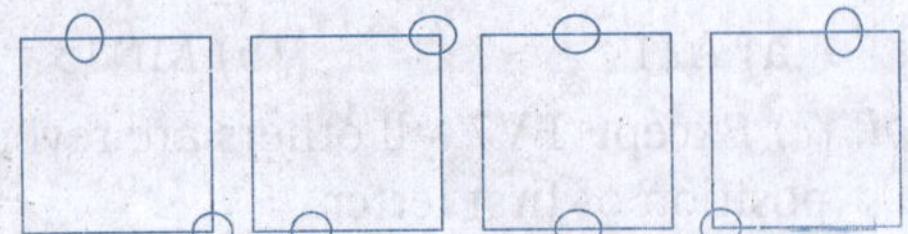

(a) (b) (c) (d)

14. Find the odd figure.

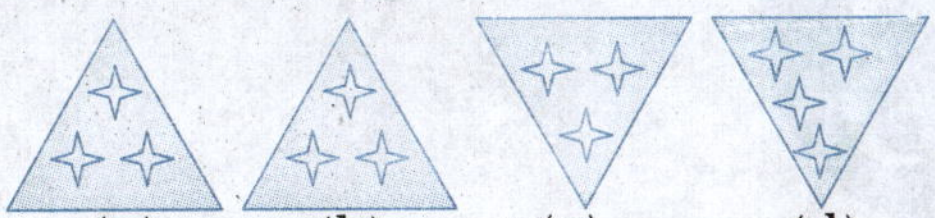

(a) (b) (c) (d)

15. Which of the following mango is odd one out.

(a) 35 (b) 99 (c) 75 (d) 36

16. Which number is different from others?

(a) 3 (b) 7 (c) 5 (d) 6

17. Find the odd one.

(a) 12 (b) 34 (c) 56 (d) 74

18. Find the odd one out.

(a) 16 (b) 4 (c) 12 (d) 19

19. Choose the odd one out.

(a) 4, 0 (b) 1, 00

(c) 3, 0 (d) 4, 0

20. Choose the odd one out?

(a) 2002 (b) 2009 (c) 2008 (d) 2022

21. From the numbers given below choose the one which is different from others.

(a) 85 (b) 76 (c) 98 (d) 49

22. Find odd one out.

(a) 44 (b) 82 (c) 73 (d) 28

23. Find odd one out.

(a) 5 (b) 7 (c) 6 (d) 2

24. Find odd one out.

(a) 12 (b) 120 (c) 38 (d) 60

25. Four group of letters are given. Choose the one which is different from others

(a) B (b) D (c) J (d) S

26. Choose the odd one.

(a) FED (b) JKI

(c) ONM (d) RQP

Chapter

03

What Comes Next?

'What Comes Next' means finding the next or missing term/figure in a given arrangement of terms/figures.

EXAMPLE 1 The figures given below are arranged according to a pattern. Find the rule followed in the pattern and select the missing figure.

?

(a)  (b)  (c)  (d) 

Sol. *(c)* Each figure repeats itself after a figure.

So, the missing figure will be as shown in option figure (c).

Hence, option (c) is correct.

EXAMPLE 2 What comes next in the series given below?

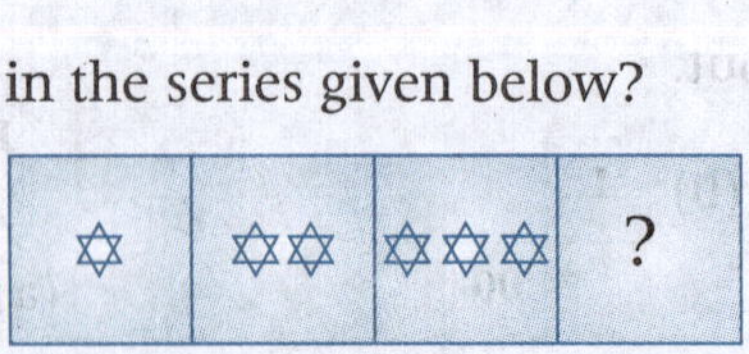

(a)  (b)  (c)  (d) 

Sol. *(a)* Stars are increasing by one in each step.

So, the next figure will be as shown in option figure (a).

Hence, option (a) is correct.

EXAMPLE 3 Find the next number in the series given below.

(a) 12 (b) 14 (c) 16 (d) 15

Sol. *(d)* Here, 2 is added to each number to obtain the next number.

$$5 \xrightarrow{+2} 7 \xrightarrow{+2} 9 \xrightarrow{+2} 11 \xrightarrow{+2} 13 \xrightarrow{+2} \boxed{15}$$

So, the next number is 15.

Hence, option (d) is correct.

EXAMPLE 4 Find the next letter in the series given below.

A, C, E, G, ?

(a) H (b) I (c) J (d) K

Sol. *(b)* $A \xrightarrow{B} C \xrightarrow{D} E \xrightarrow{F} G \xrightarrow{H} \boxed{I}$

So, the next letter is I.

Hence, option (b) is correct.

EXAMPLE 5 Find the next letter in the series given below.

(a) UV (b) VZ (c) ZX (d) ZB

Sol. *(b)* The pattern is as follows:

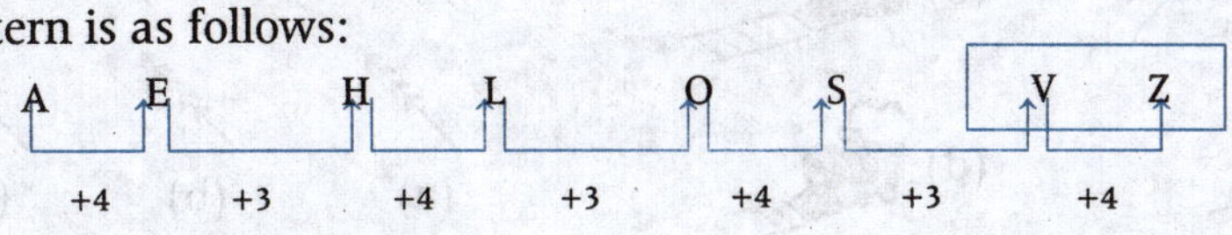

So, the missing letters are VZ.

Let's Practice

1. What comes next in the series given below?

 ?

(a)

(b)

(c)

(d)

2. Find the missing figure in the following series.

 ?

(a)

(b)

(c)

(d)

3. Find the next figure in the series given below.

 ?

(a) 

(b) 

(c) 

(d) 

4. Find the next figure in the series given below.

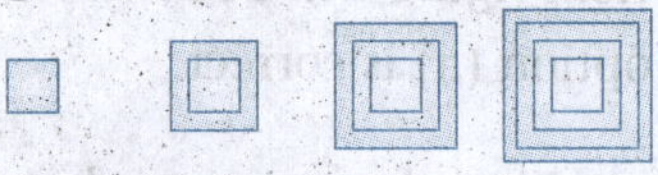 ?

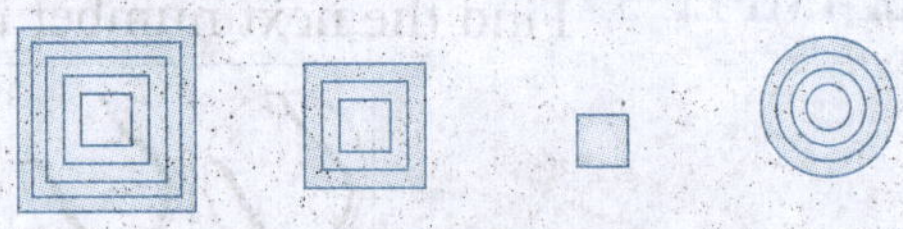
(a) (b) (c) (d)

5. Which option figure will come in the place of question mark (?).

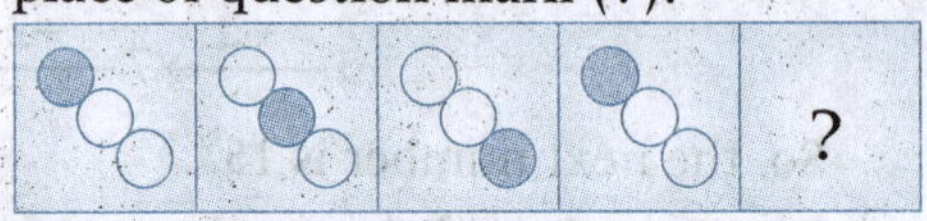

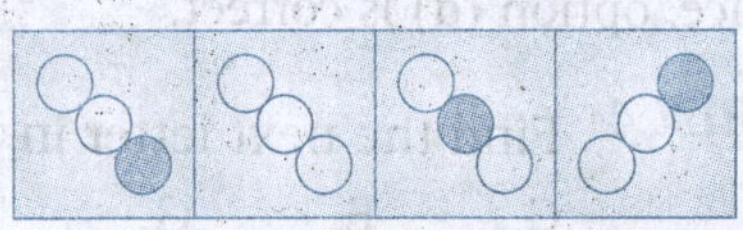
(a) (b) (c) (d)

6. Which figure will replace the question mark (?).

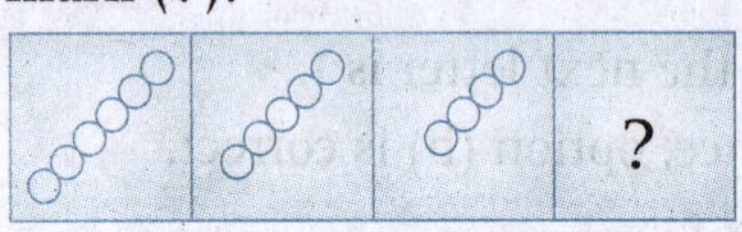

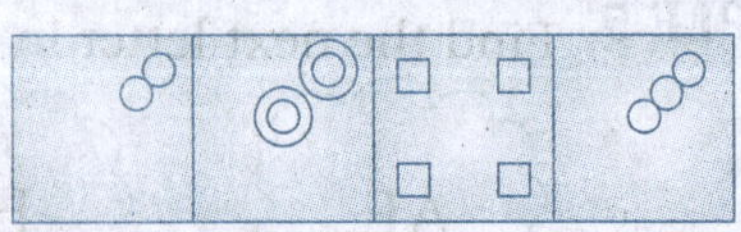
(a) (b) (c) (d)

7. Find the next figure in the following series.

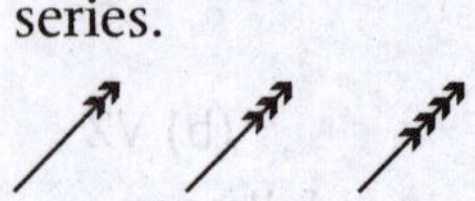 ?

(a) (b) (c) (d)

8. What comes next in the series given below?

?

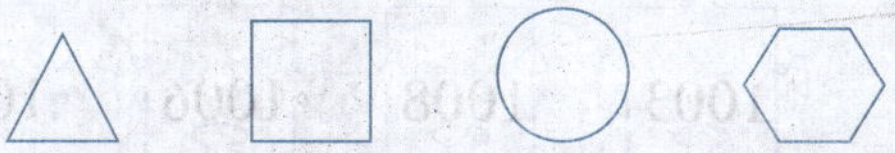

(a) (b) (c) (d)

9. Find the figure which replaces the question mark (?) and complete the series given below.

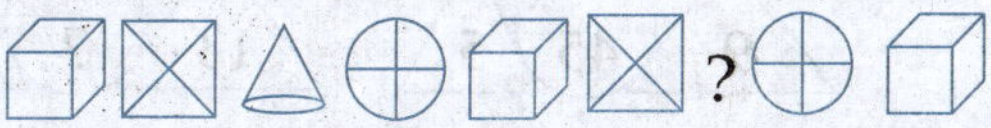

(a)

(b)

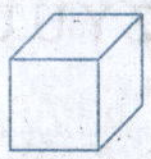

(c)

(d)

10. Find the missing figure in the following series.

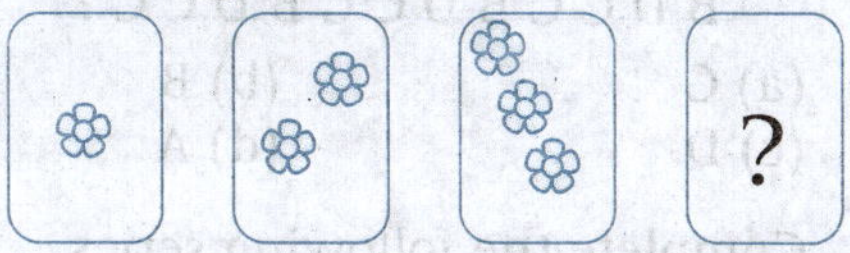

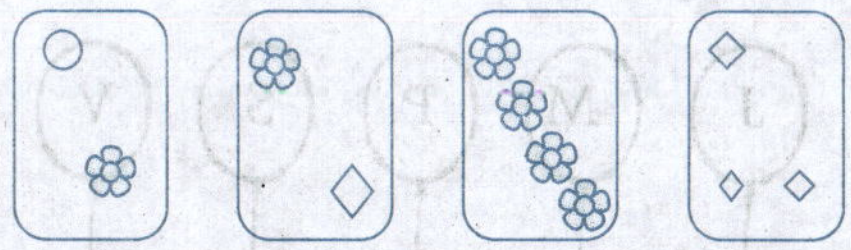

(a) (b) (c) (d)

11. What comes next in the series given below?

?

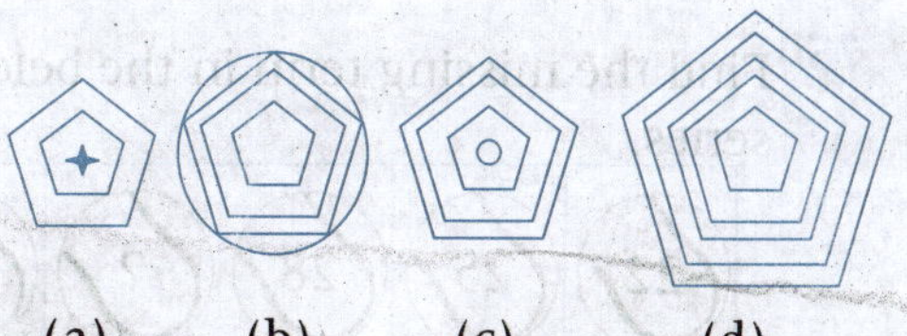

(a) (b) (c) (d)

12. Find the next figure in the series given below?

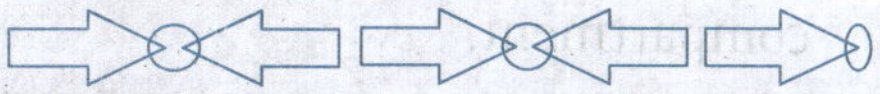

?

(a) (b) (c) (d)

13. Find the missing figure in the following series.

?

(a) (b) (c) (d)

14. Which option figure will come in the place of question mark when you start to draw a mango?

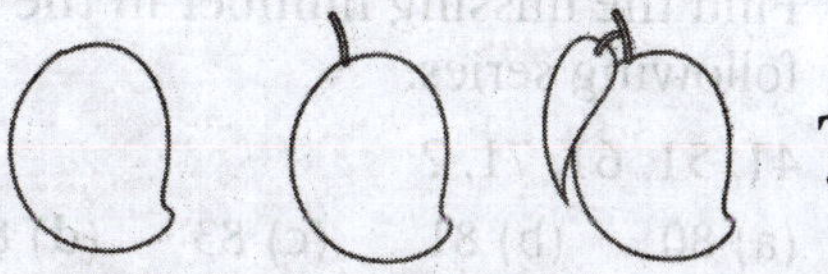

?

(I) (II) (III)

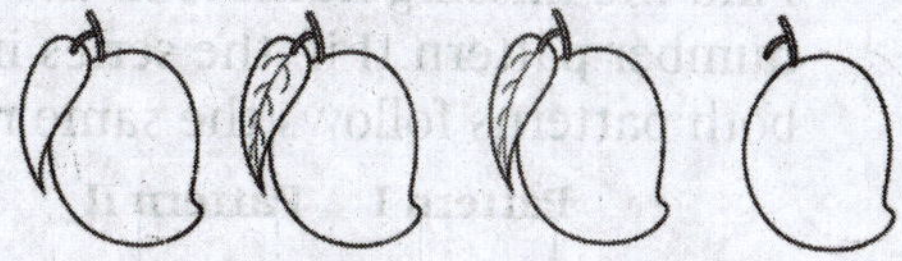

(a) (b) (c) (d)

15. Find the missing number?

6 1 2 3 6 1 2 3 6 1 2 ?

(a) 3 (b) 2

(c) 6 (d) 1

16. Find the missing term in the below series.

(a) 31 (b) 32 (c) 30 (d) 35

17. Find the missing number on the compartment.

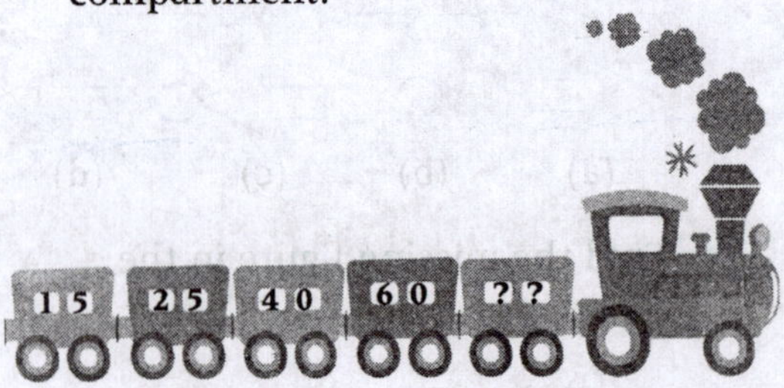

(a) 65 (b) 70 (c) 90 (d) 85

18. Find the next number in the series given below.

02	04	03	09	04	?

08	12	16	20
(a)	(b)	(c)	(d)

19. Find the missing number in the following series.

41, 51, 61, 71, ?

(a) 80 (b) 81 (c) 83 (d) 84

20. Find the missing number in the number pattern II if, the series in the both patterns follows the same rule.

Pattern I	Pattern II
81	28
92	39
103	?

(a) 30 (b) 40 (c) 45 (d) 50

21. Complete the following series?

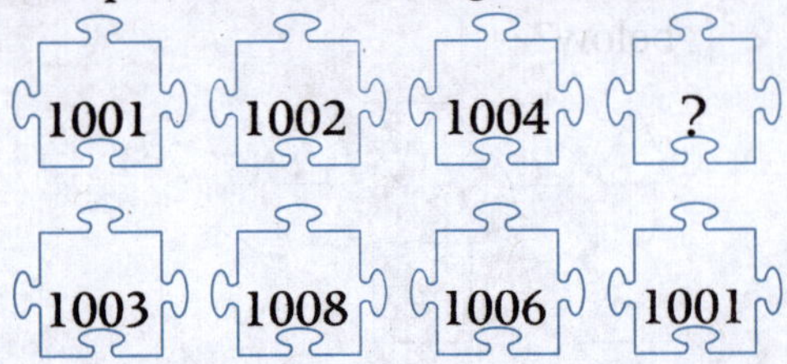

(a) (b) (c) (d)

22. Which number will come in the place of question mark(?)?

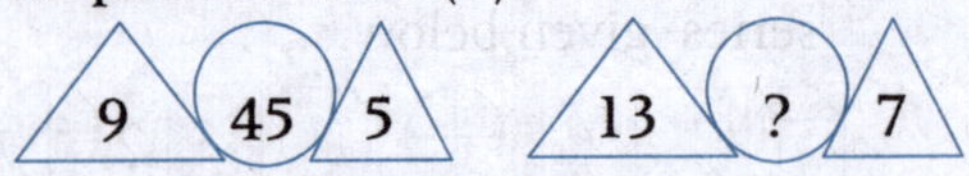

(a) 90 (b) 91 (c) 78 (d) 65

23. Find the next letter in the series given below.

X Y Z Y U U X Y Z Y U U X Y Z Y U U X ?

(a) X (b) Y
(c) Z (d) U

24. What comes next in the following series?

B D C C B D C C B D C C ?

(a) C (b) B
(c) D (d) A

25. Complete the following series.

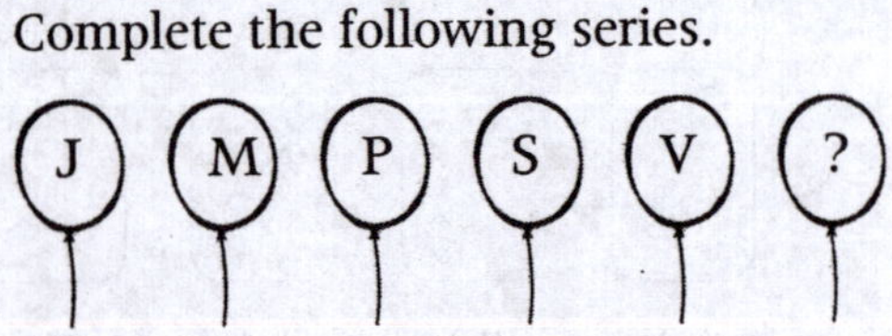

(a) X (b) W
(c) Y (d) Z

26. Which come next in the following letter series ?

IJ	MN	QR	?

(a) YZ (b) UV
(c) ST (d) WX

Chapter

04

Coding-Decoding

In this chapter, some figures, shapes, words, letters or numbers are replaced with other figures, shapes, words, letters or numbers as a code. Students are asked to find out the code for another term based on the given pattern.

EXAMPLE 1 If AB is coded as BA and CD is coded as DC, then find the code for EF.

(a) AK (b) DM (c) TL (d) FE

Sol. *(d)* As, A B ⟶ B A and C D ⟶ D C, Similarly, E F ⟶ F E

Hence, option (d) is correct.

EXAMPLE 2 If 24 is coded as 6 and 21 is coded as 3, then find the code for 25.

(a) 7 (b) 1 (c) 8 (d) 9

Sol. *(a)* As, $2+4=6$, and $2+1=3$

Similarly, $2+5=7$

Hence, option (a) is correct.

EXAMPLE 3 If  is called ,  is called  and  is called , then in which students keep books and note books.

(a) Shirt (b) Hat (c) Lunch box (d) Bag

Sol. *(c)* Students keep books in bag but here bag is called lunch box.

So, students keep books and note books in lunch box.

Hence, option (c) is correct.

Let's Practice

1. If XZ is coded as ZX and TU is coded as UT, then find the code for PQ.

(a) ZY (b) QP

(c) TA (d) BD

2. If BCD is coded as DCB, then what will be the code for NOP?

(a) NOP

(b) PON

(c) NPO

(d) ONP

3. If the code for DAR is RAD, then whatwill be the code for LAT ?

(a) TLA

(b) ALT

(c) ATL

(d) TAL

4. If PQR is coded as UVW and MNO is coded as RST, then find the code for IJK.

(a) PON (b) OPN

(c) NOP (d) QPO

5. If GIK is coded as TRP and EGI is coded as VTR, then find code for UWY.

(a) FDB (b) FDA

(c) ADF (d) BDF

6. If the code for MAN is MBO and CAN is CBO, then find the code for VAN.

(a) BOW (b) VBO

(c) WBO (d) UBO

7. If 249 is coded as 942 and 301 is coded as 103, then find the code for 796.

(a) 976 (b) 697

(c) 769 (d) 679

8. If 73 is coded as 10 and 71 is coded as 8. Then what is the code for 81?

(a) 9 (b) 4

(c) 6 (d) 3

9. If 82 is coded as 6 and 43 is coded as 1. Then what is the code for 64?

(a) 4 (b) 2

(c) 6 (d) 8

10. If 100 is coded as 11001 and 200 is coded as 22002, then find the code for 300.

(a) 83003 (b) 33300

(c) 30303 (d) 33003

11. If 8 is coded as 80×160 and 6 is coded as 60×120, then find the code for 4.

(a) 80×40 (b) 40×80

(c) 80×80 (d) 40×40

12. If 2002 is coded as 0220 and 5005 is as 0550 then, find the code for 9009.

(a) 0990 (b) 0099
(c) 9900 (d) 9090

13. If Green is called White, then what is the colour of grass?

(a) Red (b) Black
(c) Green (d) White

14. If Sunday is called Monday, and Monday is called Tuesday, then which day comes after Saturday ?

(a) Monday (b) Sunday
(c) Tuesday (d) Wednesday

15. If Apple is called Mango, and Mango is called Orange, then which fruit has yellow colour?

(a) Mango (b) Orange
(c) Apple (d) Grapes

16. If knife is called vegetable and vegetable is called fruits, then from which we cut the vegetable?

(a) Knife (b) Vegetable
(c) Fruit (d) Table

17. If 'Lotus' is called 'Rose' and 'Rose' is called 'Lily', then which is our national flower?

(a) Rose (b) Lotus
(c) Lily (d) Sunflower

18. If Door is called Bed and Bed is called Carpet, then on which a person sleeps?

(a) Carpet (b) Sofa
(c) Door (d) Bed

19. If Eraser is called Notebook, and Notebook is called Pen, then on which we write?

(a) Eraser (b) Notebook
(c) Pen (d) Pencil

20. If PINK is called Q@#L and SINK is called T@#L, then what is the code for DINE ?

(a) E@#G (b) F#@E
(c) E#@F (d) E@#F

21. Observe the following table and answer the given question

G	O	A	Q	I	N
@	3	1	m	#	p

What is the code for GAIN?

(a) p31m (b) @3#p
(c) @1#p (d) #1p@

Chapter 05

Complete the Figure

In 'complete the figure', a set of figures, numbers or letters is given. Students have to find the missing figure or term to complete the given pattern.

EXAMPLE 1 Choose the figure which will complete the following pattern.

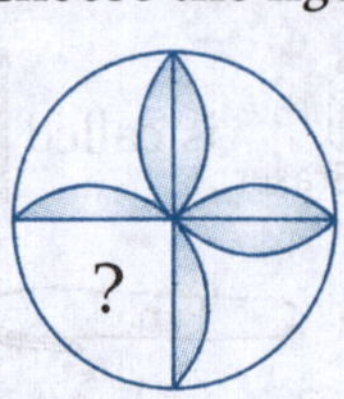

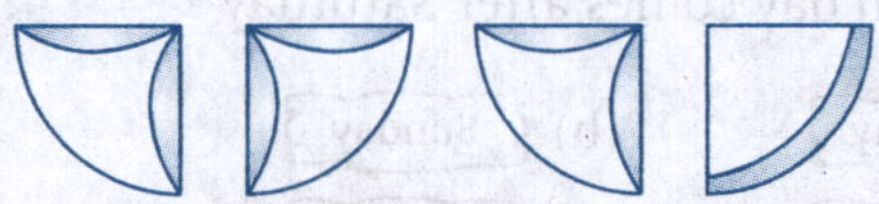

(a) (b) (c) (d)

Sol. *(a)* The pattern can be completed as

Hence, option (a) is correct.

EXAMPLE 2 Which figure from the given alternatives will complete the below pattern?

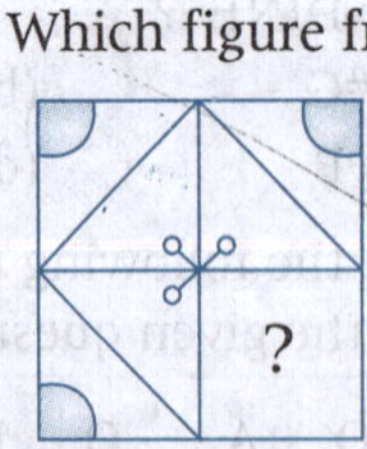

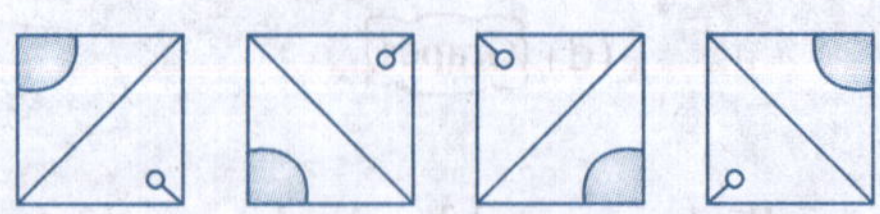

(a) (b) (c) (d)

Sol. *(c)* The given pattern can be completed as

Hence, option (c) is correct.

Let's Practice

1. Choose the figure which will complete the following pattern.

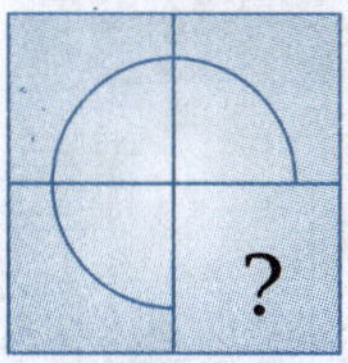

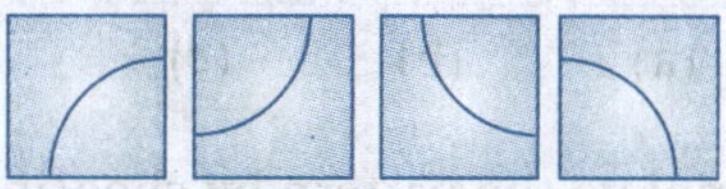

(a) (b) (c) (d)

2. Which figure from the given alternatives will complete the below pattern?

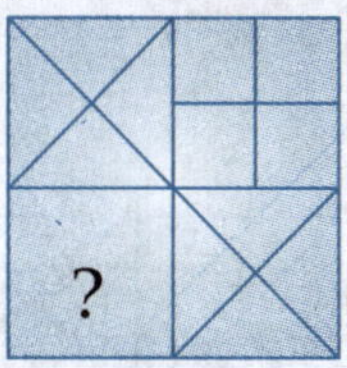

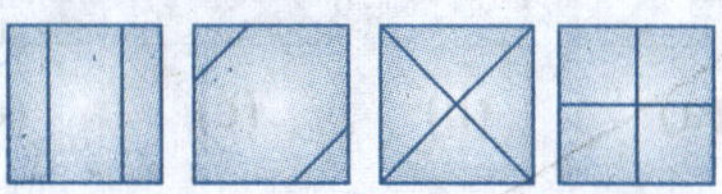

(a) (b) (c) (d)

3. Complete the pattern below by choosing the correct figure.

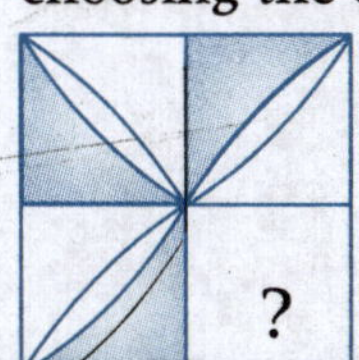

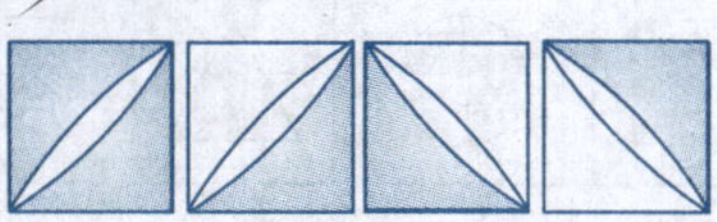

(a) (b) (c) (d)

4. Which figure will complete the below pattern?

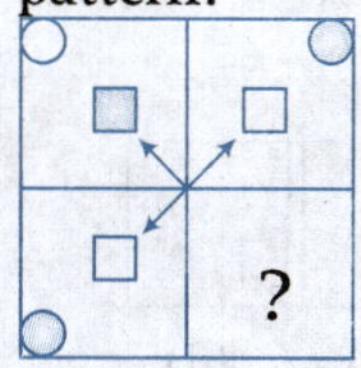

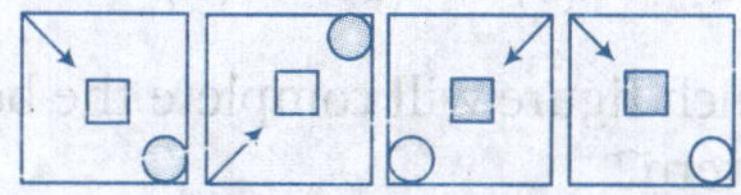

(a) (b) (c) (d)

5. Choose the figure that will complete the below pattern.

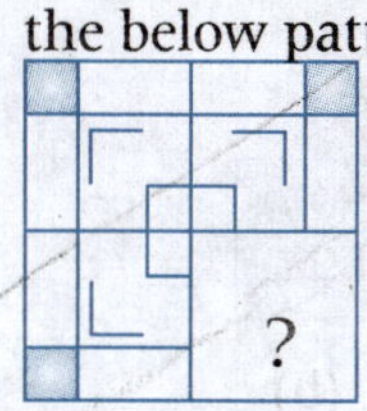

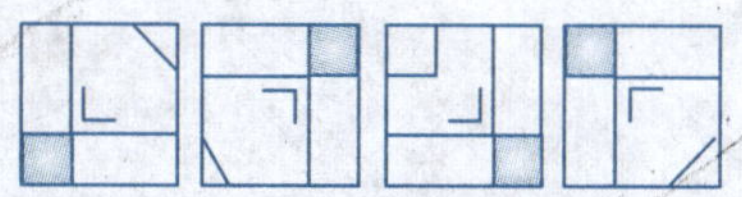

(a) (b) (c) (d)

6. Select the figure from the given alternatives that will complete the below pattern.

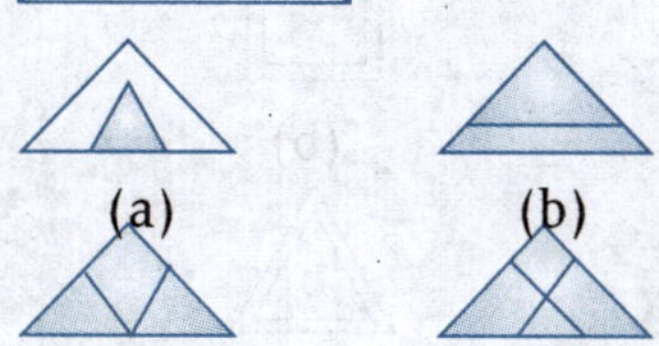

(a) (b)

(c) (d)

7. Complete the pattern by choosing the correct figure.

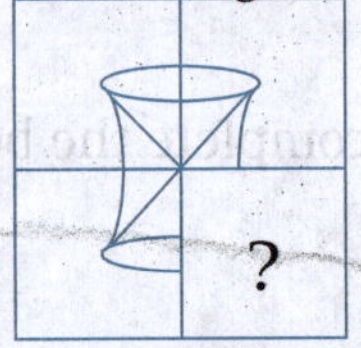

(a) (b) (c) (d)

8. Which figure will complete the below pattern?

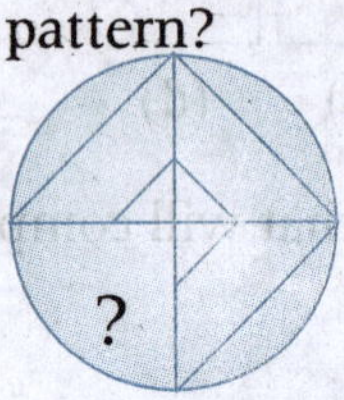

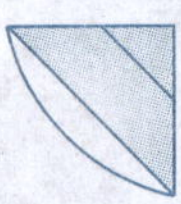

(a)

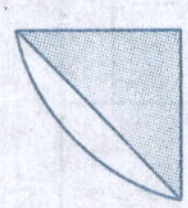

(b)

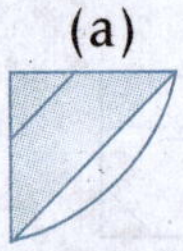

(c)

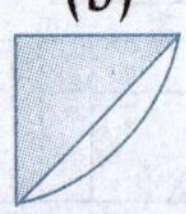

(d)

9. Complete the pattern by choosing the correct figure.

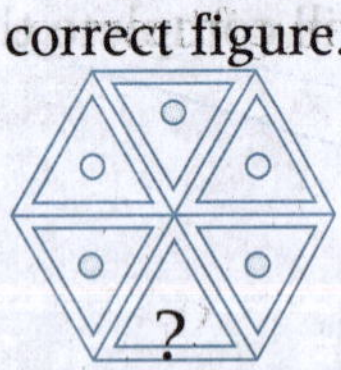

(a)

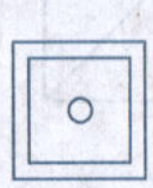

(b)

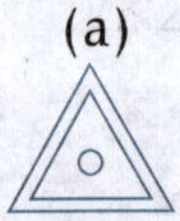

(c)

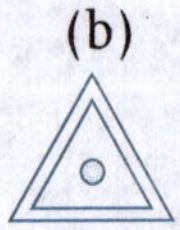

(d)

10. Complete the pattern by choosing the correct figure.

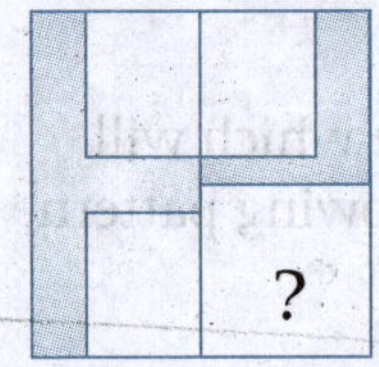

(a) (b) (c) (d)

11. Complete the pattern by choosing the correct figure.

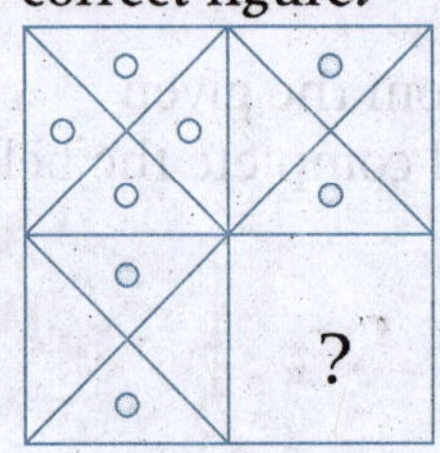

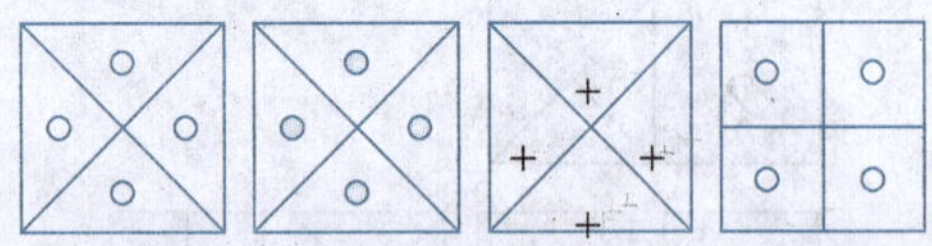

(a) (b) (c) (d)

12. Complete the pattern by choosing the correct figure.

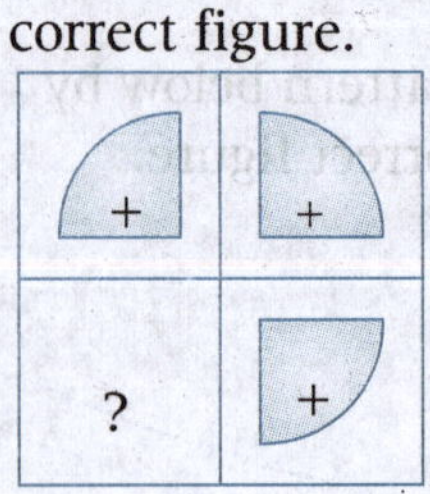

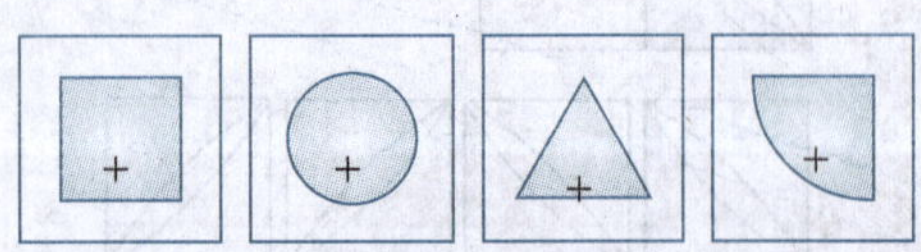

(a) (b) (c) (d)

13. Which figure will complete the below pattern (?)

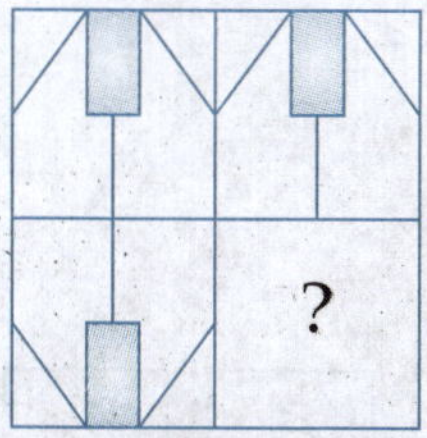

(a) (b) (c) (d)

14. Complete the pattern by choosing the correct figure.

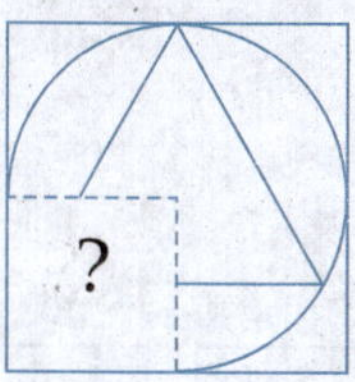

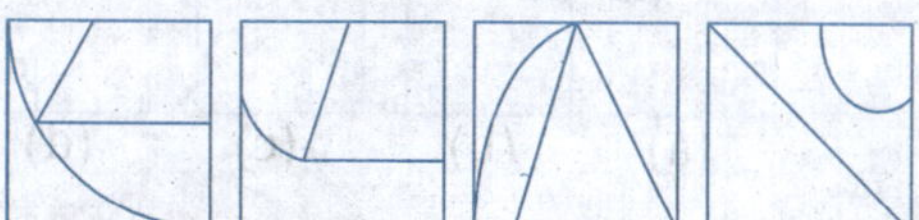

(a) (b) (c) (d)

15. Choose figure from the given alternatives that will complete the below pattern?

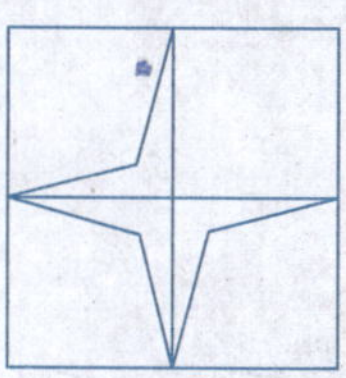

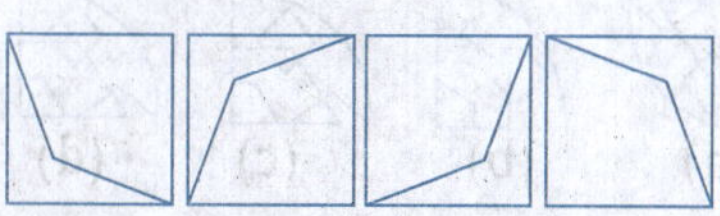

(a) (b) (c) (d)

16. Which figure from the given alternatives will complete the below pattern?

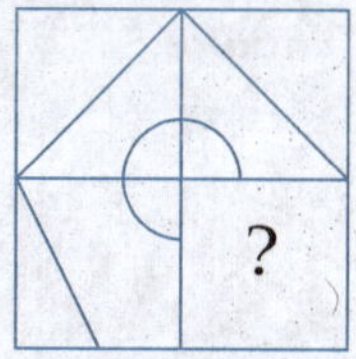

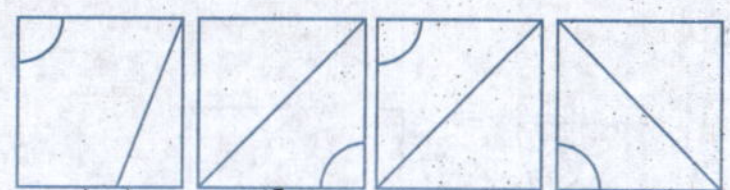

(a) (b) (c) (d)

17. Which figure from the given alternatives will complete the below pattern?

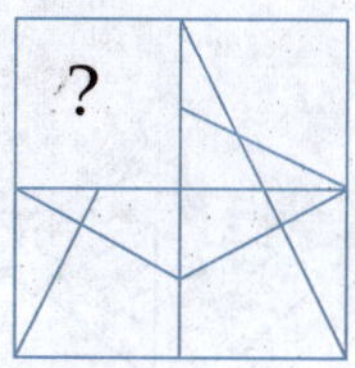

(a) (b) (c) (d)

18. Select the figure from the given alternatives that will complete the below pattern?

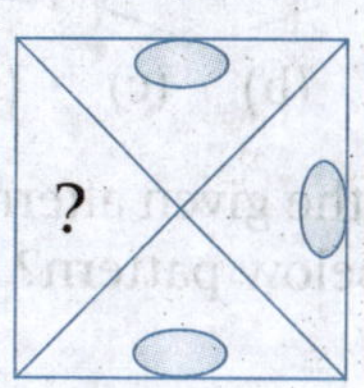

(a) (b) (c) (d)

19. Choose figure from the given alternatives will complete the below pattern.

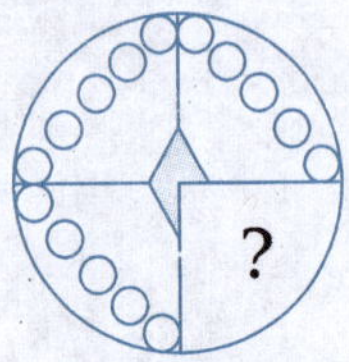

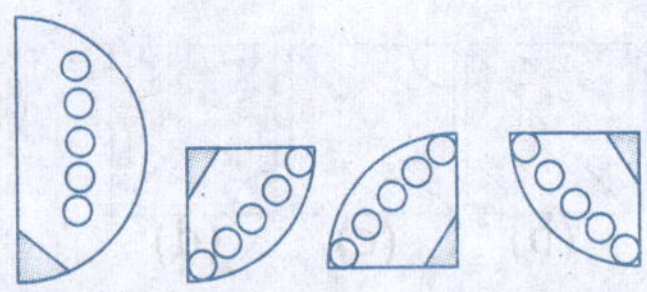

(a) (b) (c) (d)

20. Which figure from the given alternatives will complete the below pattern?

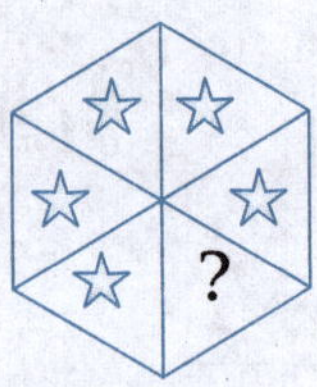

(a) (b) (c) (d)

21. Complete the pattern by choosing the correct figure?

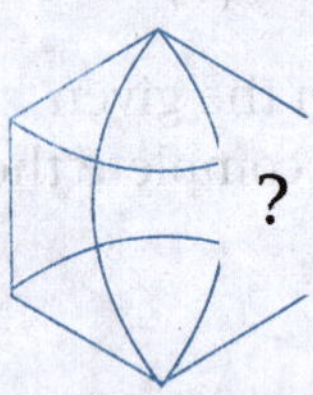

(a) (b) (c) (d)

22. Which figure from the given alternatives will complete the below pattern?

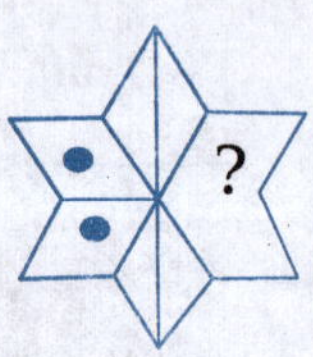

(a) (b) (c) (d)

23. Complete the pattern by choosing the correct figure.

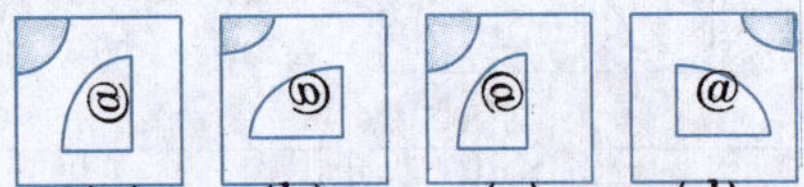

(a) (b) (c) (d)

24. Which figure from the given alternatives will complete the below pattern?

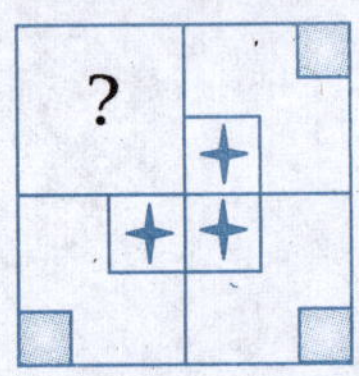

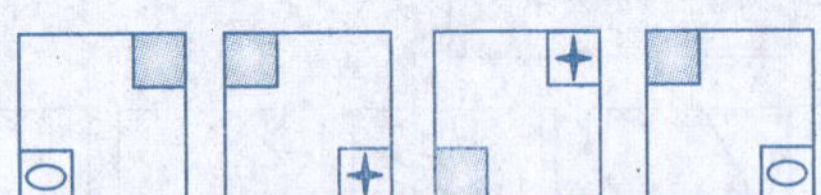

(a) (b) (c) (d)

25. Choose figure from the given alternatives will complete the below pattern.

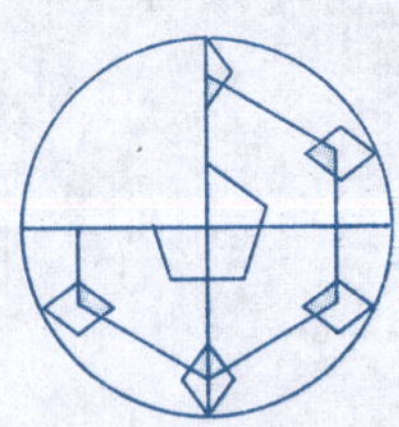

(a) (b) (c) (d)

Chapter

06

Find Similar Figure and Grouping of Figures

In 'Similar Figures', two or three shapes/pictures are given. In this type of question, a student is required to find the shape/picture having similar pattern as that of the given figures.

In 'Grouping of figures', we have to form the groups of certain number of figures.

EXAMPLE 1 Which shape or pattern belongs to the group of shapes given below?

Question Figures

Answer Figures

(a)  (b)  (c)  (d) 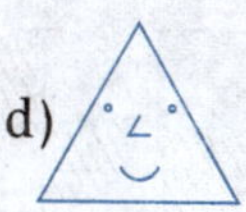

Sol. *(d)* The given two shapes have smiling face with two eyes and one nose.
The shape given in option (d) has smiling face with two eyes and one nose.
So, the shape in option (d) is similar to the given group of shapes.
Hence, option (d) is correct.

EXAMPLE 2 How many groups of 3 butterflies can be formed?

(a) 3 (b) 4 (c) 5 (d) 6

Sol. *(c)*

So, 5 groups of 3 butterflies can be formed from the given figures.
Hence, option (c) is correct.

Let's Practice

1. Which shape or pattern belongs to the group of shapes given below?

Question Figures

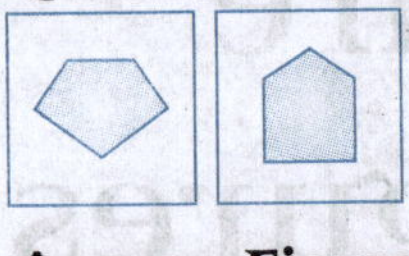

Answer Figures

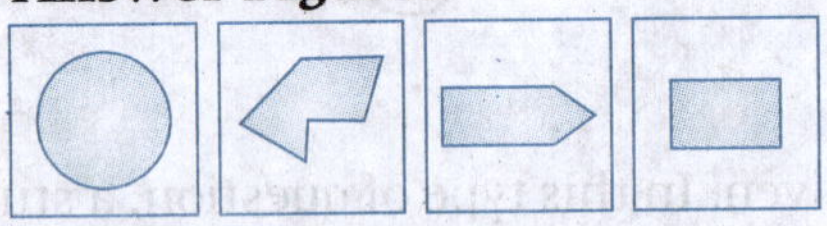

(a) (b) (c) (d)

2. Which shape or pattern belongs to the given group of shapes?

Question Figures

Answer Figures

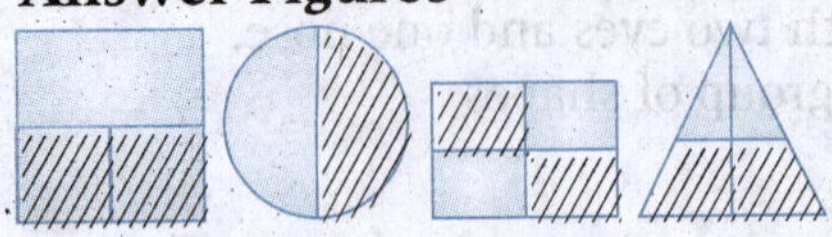

(a) (b) (c) (d)

3. Which shape is similar to the following group of two shapes?

Question Figures

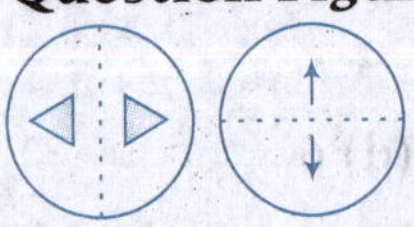

Answer Figures

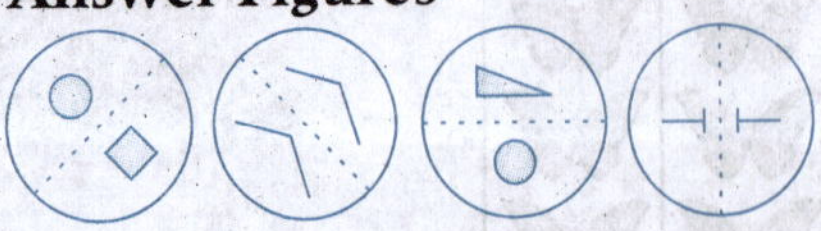

(a) (b) (c) (d)

4. Which shape or pattern belongs to the group of shapes given below?

Question Figures

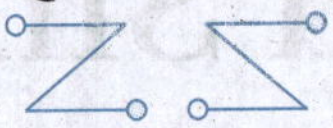

Answer Figures

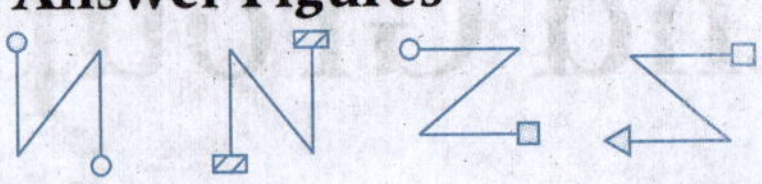

(a) (b) (c) (d)

5. Which shape is similar to the given group of shapes?

Question Figures

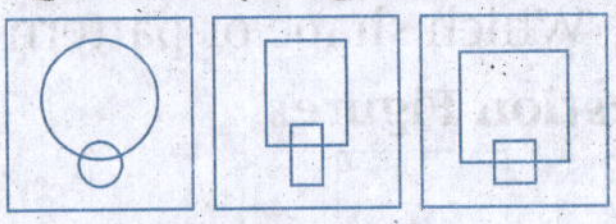

Answer Figures

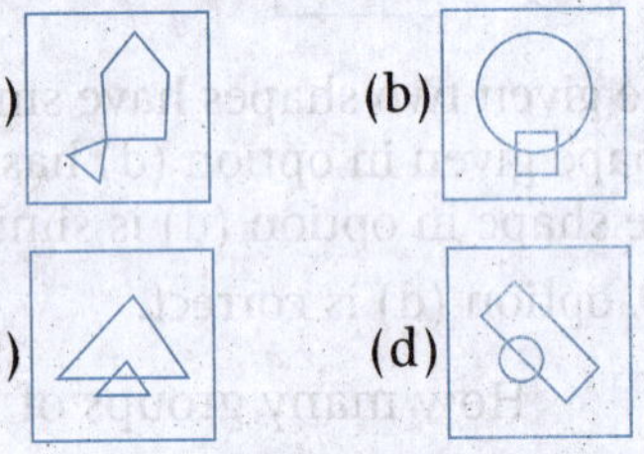

(a) (b) (c) (d)

6. Which of the following shape is similar to the given group of shapes?

Question Figures

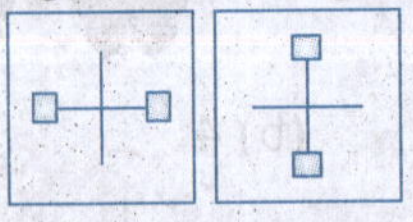

Answer Figures

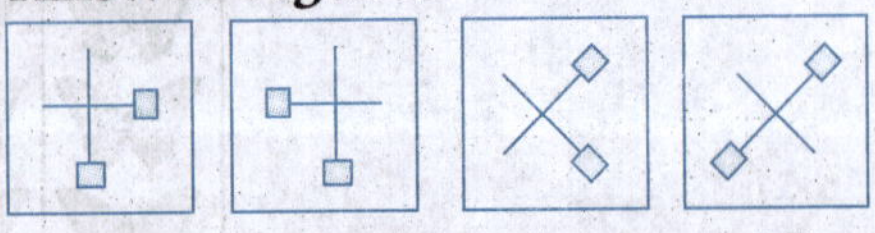

(a) (b) (c) (d)

7. Choose the shape which is similar to the given group of shapes.

Question Figures

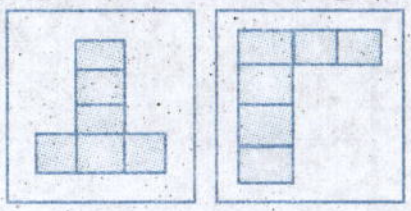

Answer Figures

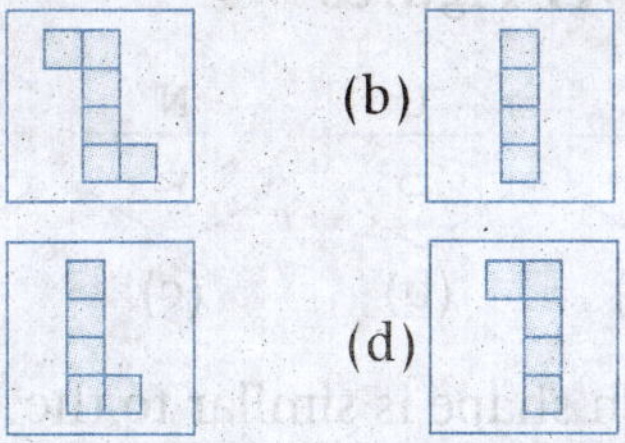

(a) (b) (c) (d)

8. Select the figure which is similar to the given group of figures.

Question Figures

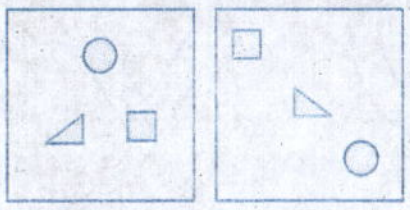

Answer Figures

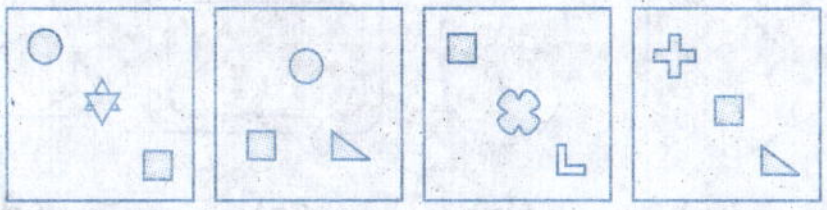

(a) (b) (c) (d)

9. Which figure is similar to the given group of shapes?

Question Figures

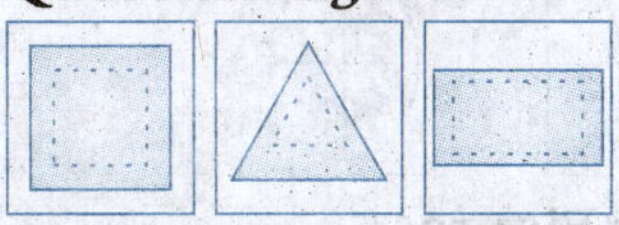

Answer Figures

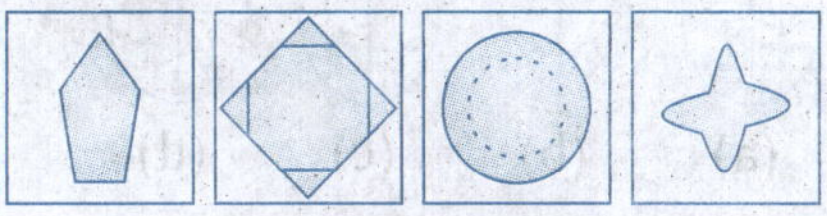

(a) (b) (c) (d)

10. Find the figure which is similar to the given group of shapes.

Question Figures

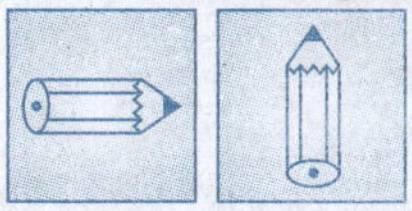

Answer Figures

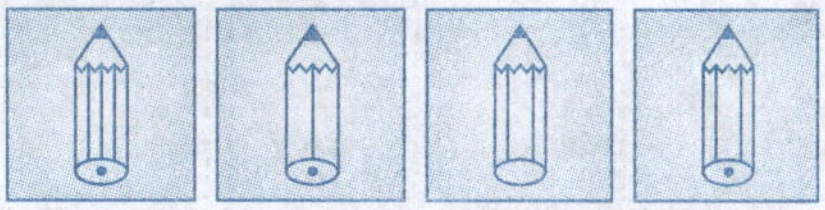

(a) (b) (c) (d)

11. Which of the following shape is similar to the given group of shapes?

Question Figures

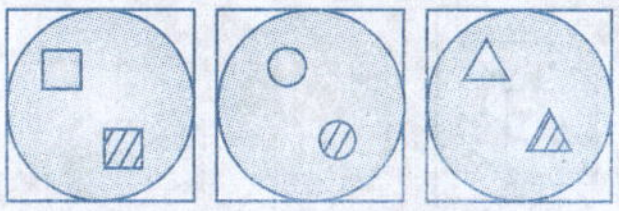

Answer Figures

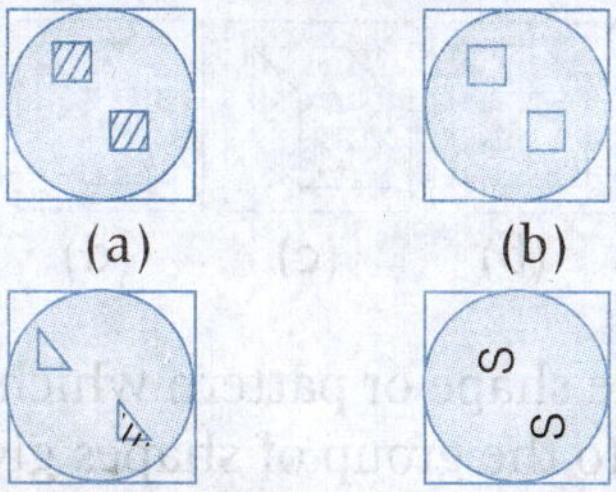

(a) (b) (c) (d)

12. Choose the shape which is similar to the given shapes.

Question Figures

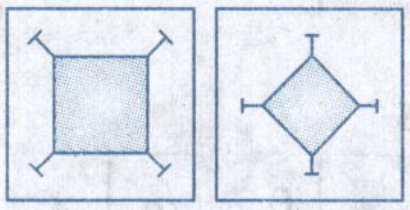

Answer Figures

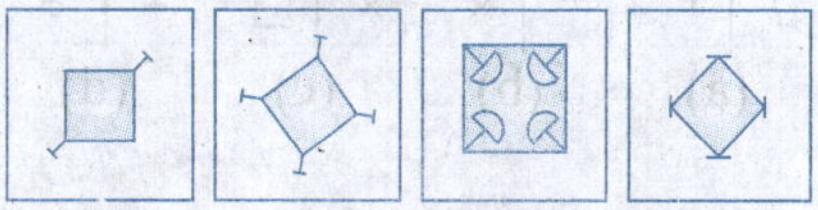

(a) (b) (c) (d)

13. Which shape is similar to the given group of shapes?

Question Figures

Answer Figures

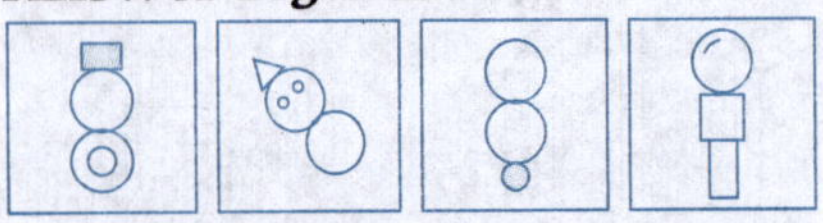

(a) (b) (c) (d)

14. Choose the shape which is similar to the given group of shapes.

Question Figures

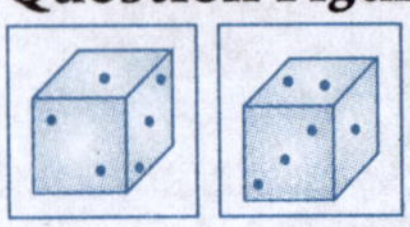

Answer Figures

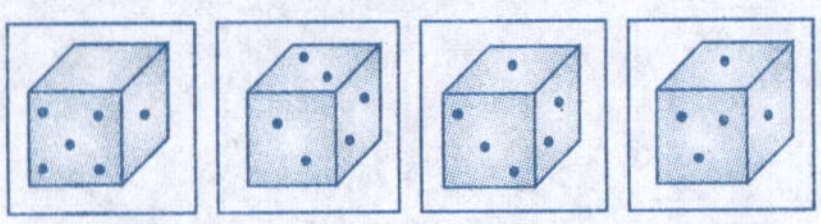

(a) (b) (c) (d)

15. Select the shape or pattern which belongs to the group of shapes given below.

Question Figures

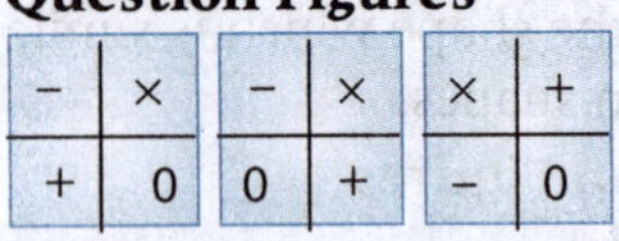

Answer Figures

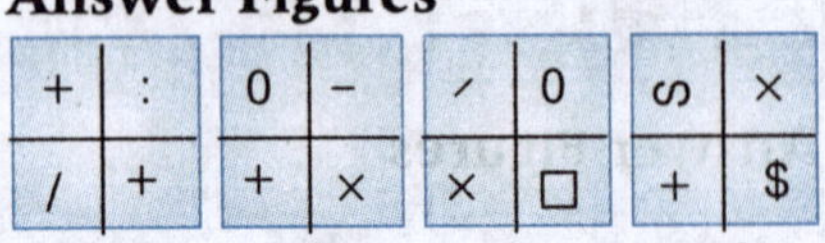

(a) (b) (c) (d)

16. Which shape is similar to the following group of two shapes?

Question Figures

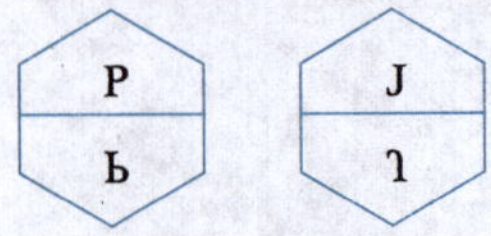

Answer Figures

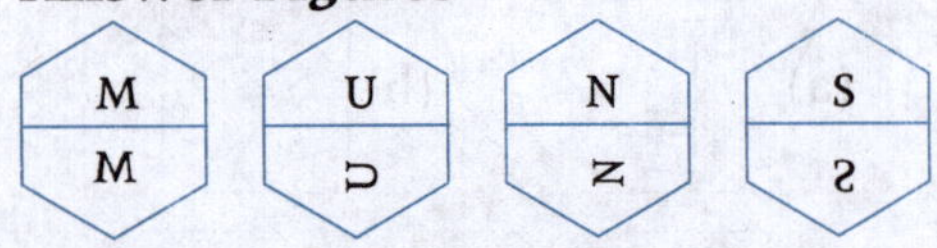

(a) (b) (c) (d)

17. Which shape is similar to the following group of two shapes?

Question Figures

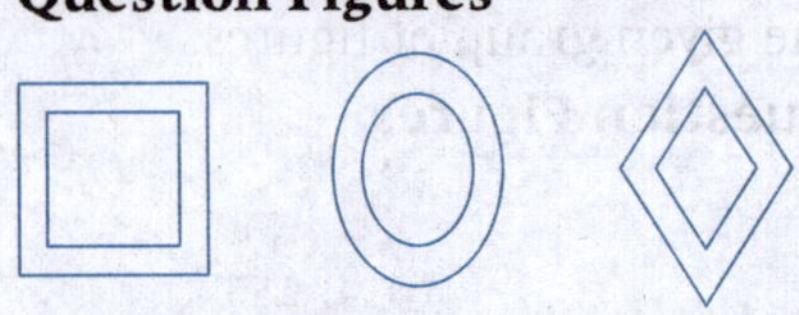

Answer Figures

(a) (b) (c) (d)

18. Which shape is similar to the following group of two shapes?

Question Figures

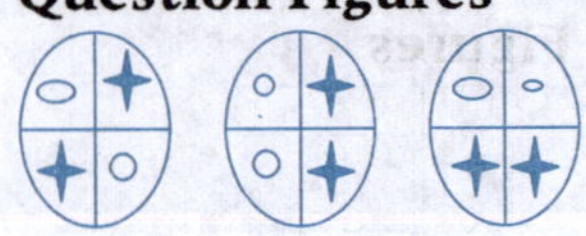

Answer Figures

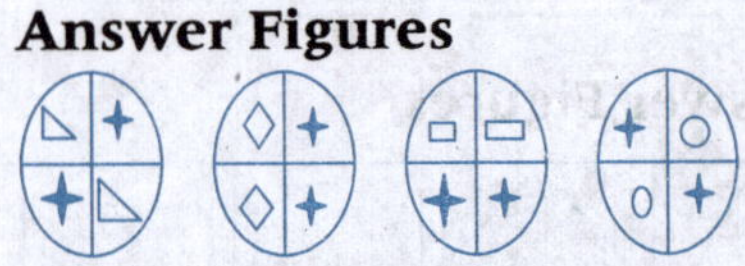

(a) (b) (c) (d)

19. Which shape is similar to the following group of two shapes?

Question Figures

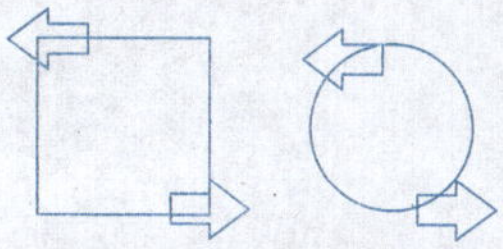

Answer Figures

(a) (b) (c) (d)

20. Which shape is similar to the following group of two shapes?

Question Figures

Answer Figures

(a) (b) (c) (d)

21. How many groups of 2 teddy bears are there?

(a) 8 (b) 4 (c) 7 (d) 6

22. Lia drew some stars as shown below.

How many stars are there in each group, if 6 groups having same number of stars are formed?

(a) 4 (b) 3 (c) 5 (d) 8

23. How many more glasses are required, if we form 4 groups of 4 glasses using given glasses?

(a) 0 (b) 1 (c) 2 (d) 3

24. Rajat put some books in his school bag shown below.

How many groups are there in each group, if 4 groups having same number of books are formed?

(a) 6 (b) 7 (c) 8 (d) 9

25. How many more birthday cap are required in a party, if we form 5 groups of 5 persons using given birthday cap?

(a) 1 (b) 2 (c) 3 (d) 4

Chapter

07

Hidden Figures

In 'Hidden Figures, we have to find out the hidden figure/shape in a given complex figure.

EXAMPLE 1 In which of the following figures, the given shape (X) is hidden?

(X)

(a)

(b)

(c)

(d)

Sol. *(b)* The given shape (X) is hidden in figure (b) as shown below.

Hence, option (b) is correct.

Direction (Ex. No. 2) Observe the figure carefully and answer the question based on it.

EXAMPLE 2 Which shape is hidden in the above figure?

(a) (b)  (c) (d)

Sol. *(b)* Shape given in option (b) is hidden in the above figure as shown below.

Hence, option (b) is correct.

EXAMPLE 3 Which of the following part is hidden in the given figure (X)?

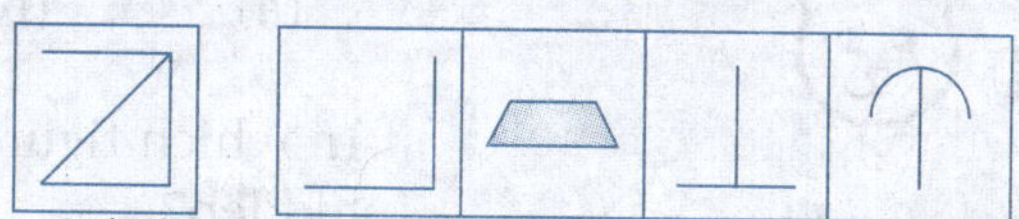

(X) (a) (b) (c) (d)

Sol. *(a)* Figure (a) is hidden in the given figure (X) as shown below figure.

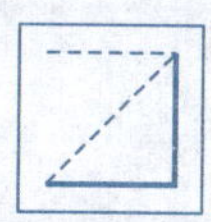

Hence, option (a) is correct.

EXAMPLE 4 Which of the following figures is hidden in the given picture?

(a) (b) (c) (d)

Sol. *(a)* Shape '' given in option (a) is hidden in the given picture.

Let's Practice

1. Tim drew a figure as shown below

Identify the figure in which the above figure is hidden.

(a) 
(b) 
(c) 
(d) 

2. Julia drew four different trains as shown below. Identify the train in which the following figure (X) is hidden.

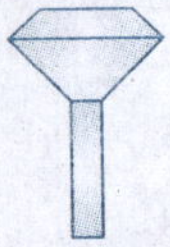

(X)

(a)

(b)

(c)

(d)

3. Kanwar drew four different mangoes as shown below. Identify the mango in which the following figure (X) is hidden.

(X)

(a)

(b)

(c)

(d)

4. Choose the figure in which the given figure (X) is hidden.

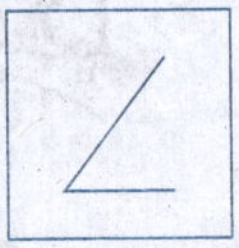

(X)

(a)

(b)

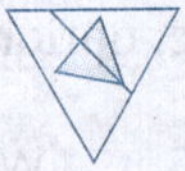
(c)

(d)

5. In which figure the given shape (X) is hidden?

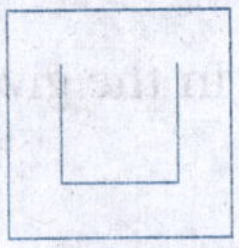

(X)

(a)

(b)

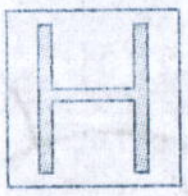
(c)

(d)

6. Choose the figure in which the given figure (X) is hidden.

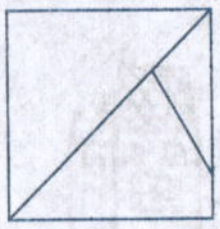

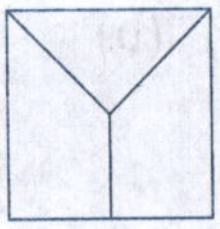
(a)

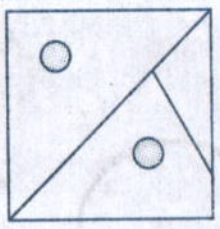
(b)

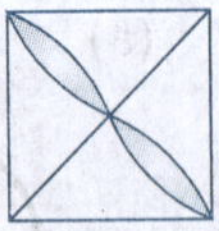
(c)

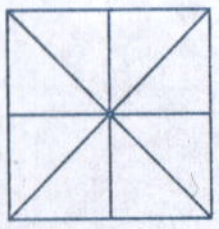
(d)

7. Identify the figure in which the given figure (X) is hidden.

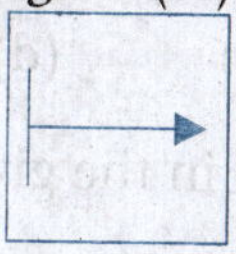

(X)

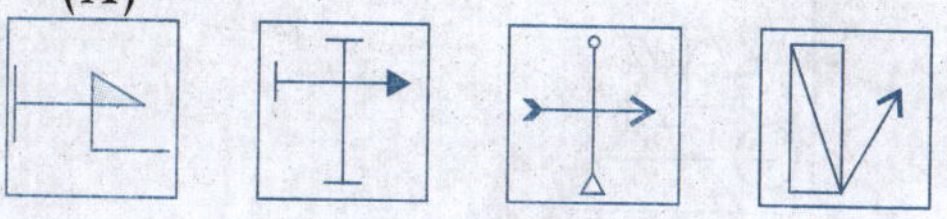

(a) (b) (c) (d)

8. Select the figure in which the given figure (X) is hidden.

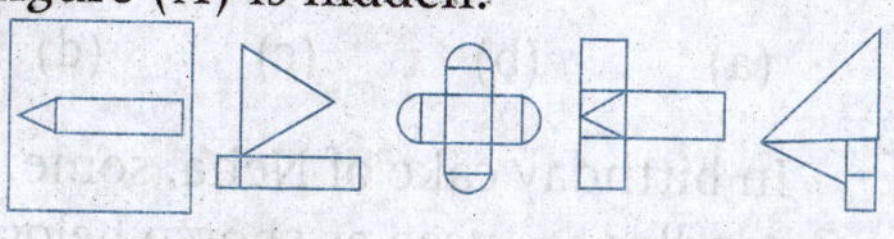

(X) (a) (b) (c) (d)

9. Which of the following part is hidden in the given figure (X)?

(X)

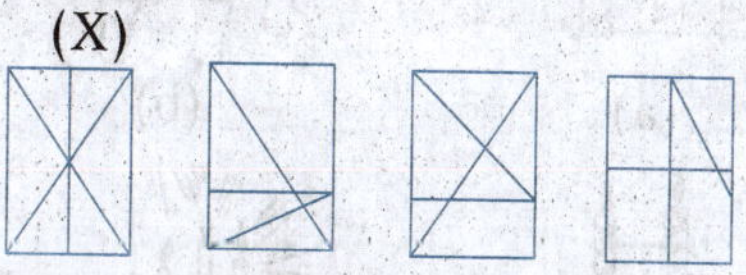

(a) (b) (c) (d)

10. In which large shape or pattern is the figure (X) is hidden?

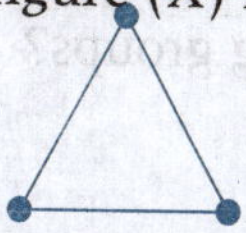

(X)

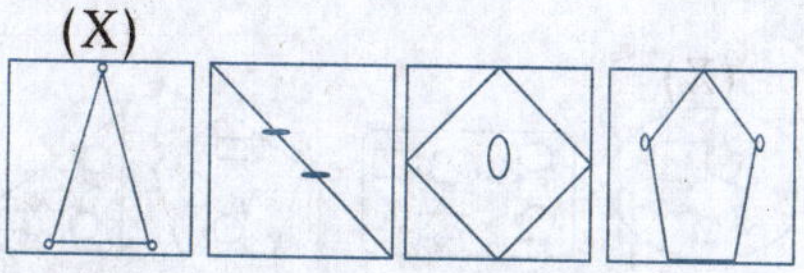

(a) (b) (c) (d)

11. Select the figure in which given figure (X) is hidden.

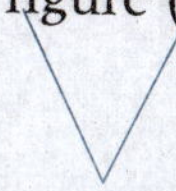

(X)

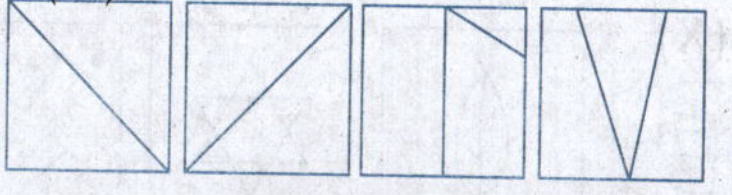

(a) (b) (c) (d)

12. In which large shape or pattern is the figure (X) is hidden?

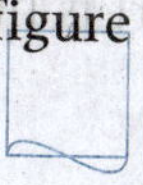

(X)

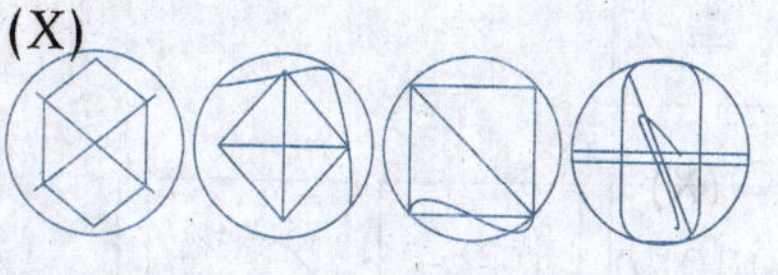

(a) (b) (c) (d)

13. Select the figure in which given figure (X) is hidden.

(X)

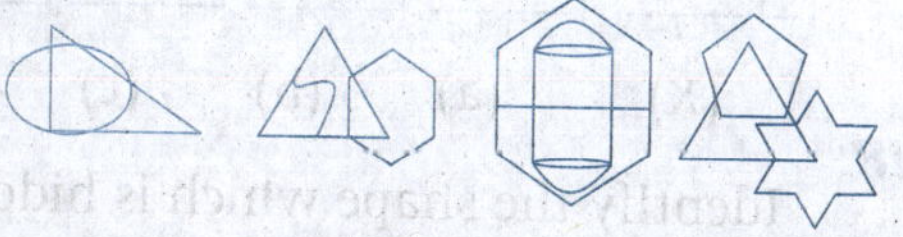

(a) (b) (c) (d)

14. Which of the following part is hidden in the given figure (X)?

(X)

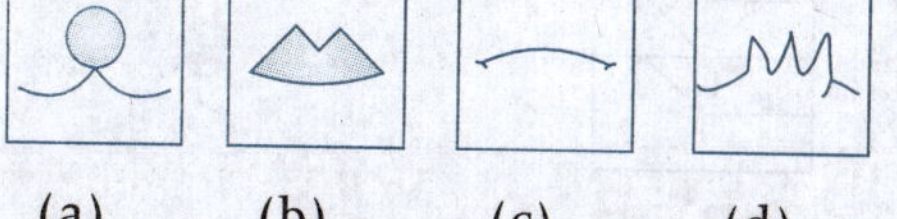

(a) (b) (c) (d)

15. Which of the following part is hidden in the given figure (X)?

(X)

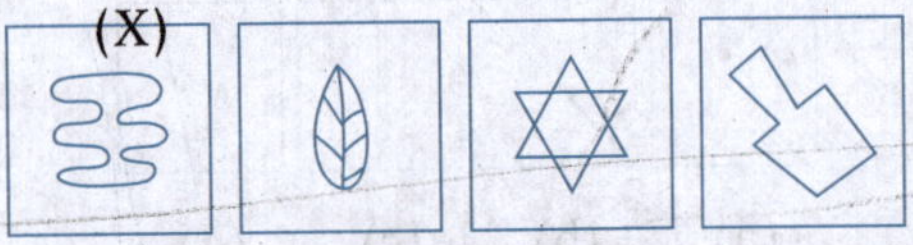

(a) (b) (c) (d)

16. Which of the following part is hidden in the given figure (X)?

(X)

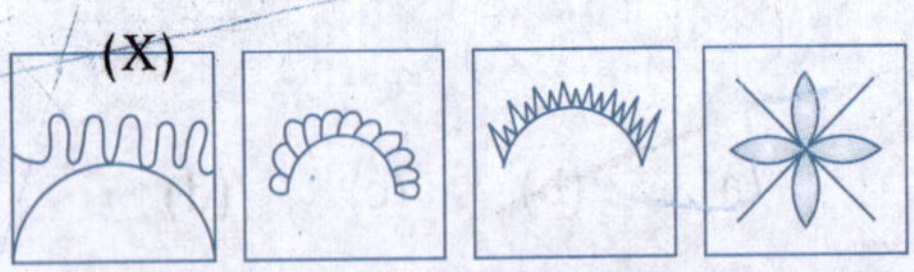

(a) (b) (c) (d)

17. Which of the following part is hidden in the given figure (X)?

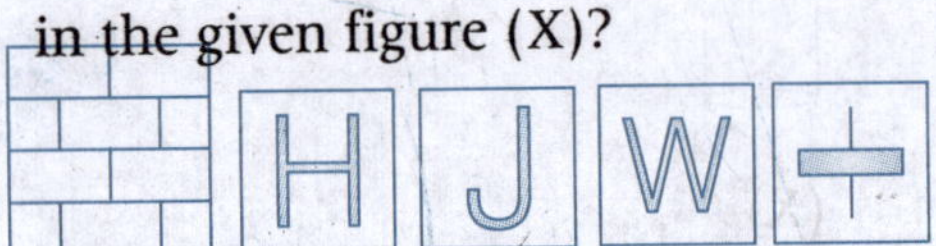

(X) (a) (b) (c) (d)

18. Identify the shape which is hidden in figure (X).

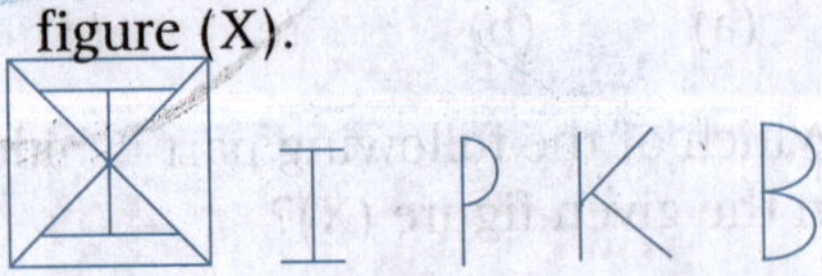

(X) (a) (b) (c) (d)

19. Which of the following figure is hidden in the given figure (X)?

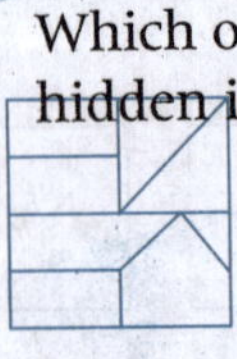

(X)

(a) (b) (c) (d)

20. Which shape is hidden in the given figure (X).

(X)

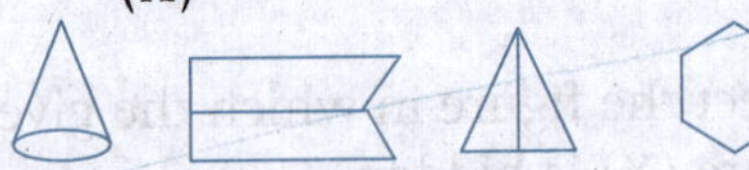

(a) (b) (c) (d)

21. In birthday cake of Neha, some candles are used as shown below.

Identify the figure in which the above figure candles is hidden.

(a)

(b)

(c)

(d)

22. Given part of the figure is hidden in which of the following groups?

(X)

(a) (b) (c) (d)

Directions (Q. Nos. 23 and 24) Observe the figure carefully and answer the questions based on it.

23. Which shape is hidden in the above figure?

(a)  (b) 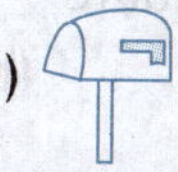 (c)  (d) 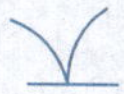

24. How many of the pictures below are hidden in the above figure?

(a) 2 (b) 3
(c) 4 (d) 1

Directions (Q. Nos. 25 and 26) Observe the picture carefully and answer the questions based on it.

25. Which shape is hidden in part '3' of the picture?

(a)  (b) 

(c)  (d) 

26. In which part of the picture is the shape '' hidden?

(a) 1 (b) 2
(c) 3 (d) 4

Direction (Q. No. 27) Observe the picture carefully and answer the question based on it.

27. How many pictures below are hidden in the given picture.

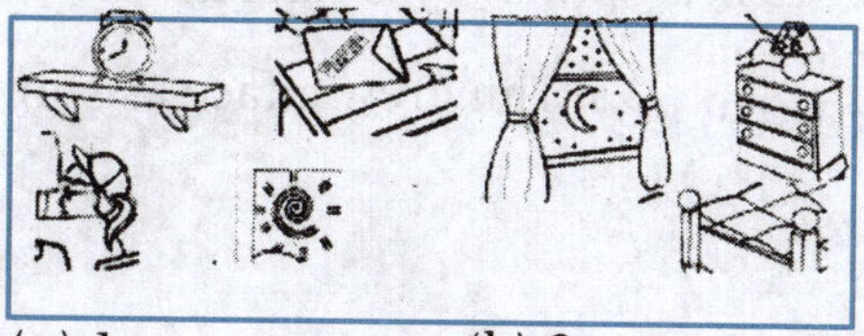

(a) 1 (b) 2
(c) 3 (d) 4

Chapter
08

Counting of Figures

This chapter deals with the questions based on geometrical shapes.

Geometrical shapes include lines, circle, square etc. Some of the geometrical shapes are given below

(i) 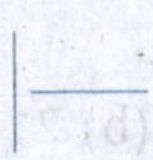 → Straight Lines

(ii) 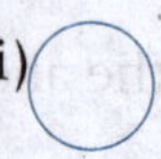 → Circle

(iii) 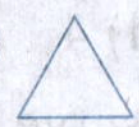 → Triangle

(iv) 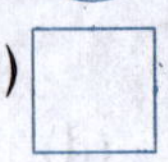 → Square

(v)  → Rectangle

EXAMPLE 1 Count the number of straight lines in the following figure.

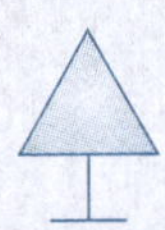

(a) 4 (b) 5 (c) 6 (d) 3

Sol. *(b)* Number of straight lines can be counted as

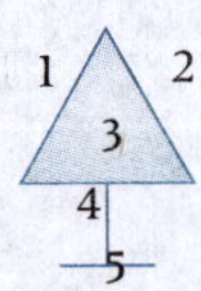

So, there are 5 straight lines in the above figure.

Hence, option (b) is correct.

EXAMPLE 2 Tim drew a face as shown below

How many squares are there in the above face?

(a) 4 (b) 3 (c) 2 (d) 5

Sol. *(a)* The given face has 4 squares as shown below

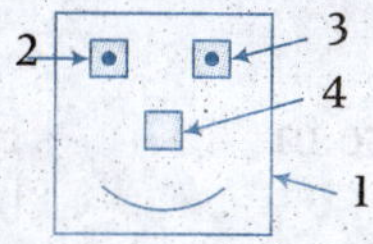

Hence, option (a) is correct.

EXAMPLE 3 Count the number of triangles in the following figure.

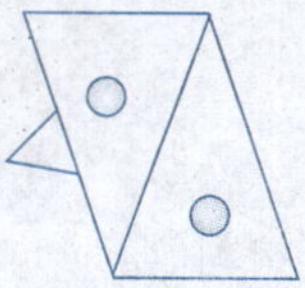

(a) 2 (b) 1 (c) 3 (d) 4

Sol. *(c)* Number of triangles can be counted as

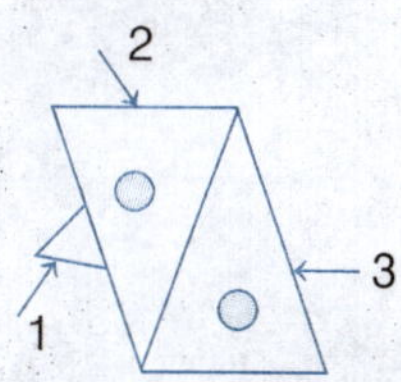

Hence, option (c) is correct.

EXAMPLE 4 Count the number of circles in the following figure.

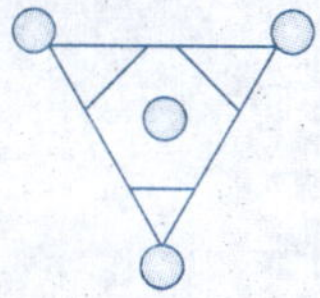

(a) 6 (b) 4 (c) 5 (d) 3

Sol. *(b)* Number of circles can be counted as

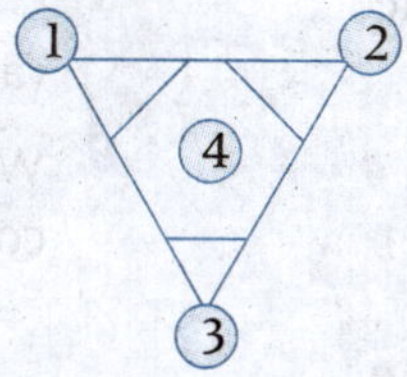

So, there are 4 circles in the above figure.

Hence, option (b) is correct.

Let's Practice

1. How many straight lines are there in below figure?

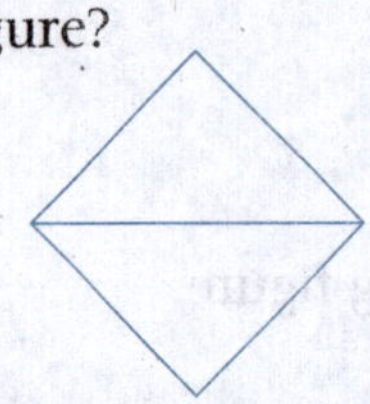

(a) 4 (b) 5
(c) 6 (d) 7

2. Count the number of straight lines in the below figure.

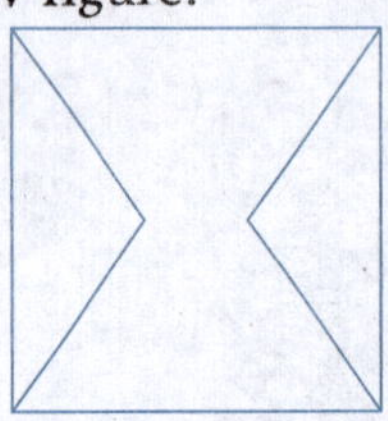

(a) 7 (b) 5
(c) 6 (d) 8

3. How many straight lines does the figure have?

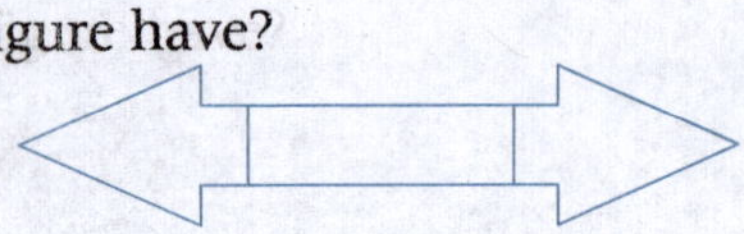

(a) 14 (b) 13
(c) 15 (d) 16

4. How many straight lines does the figure have?

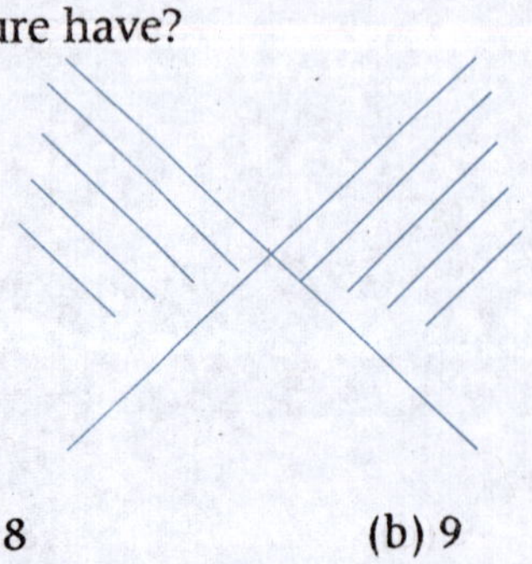

(a) 8 (b) 9
(c) 10 (d) 11

5. How many squares are there in the below figure?

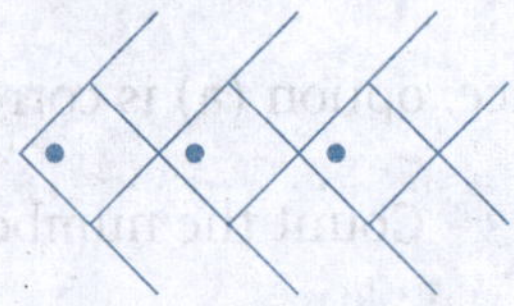

(a) 4 (b) 5 (c) 3 (d) 6

6. How many squares are there in the below figure?

(a) 5 (b) 6 (c) 7 (d) 8

7. Count the number of squares in the below figure.

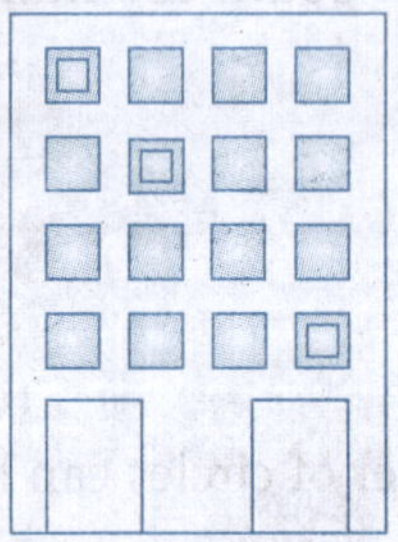

(a) 14 (b) 16 (c) 20 (d) 10

8. Which of the following figures contains exactly four squares?

(a) 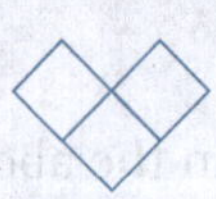 (b) 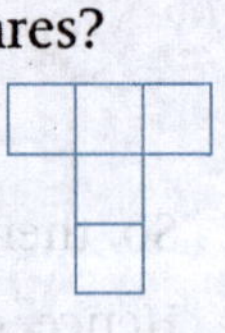

(c)  (d) 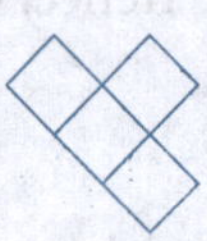

9. How many squares are there in the figure.

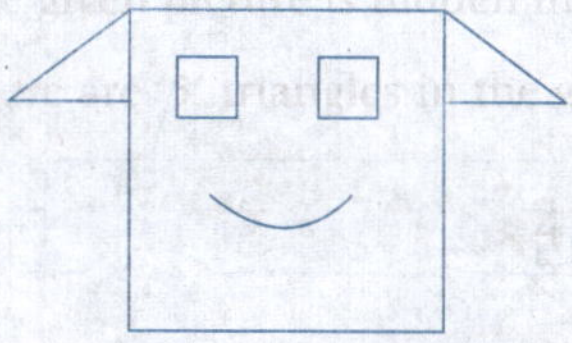

(a) 1 (b) 2
(c) 3 (d) 4

10. How many squares are present in the given figure?

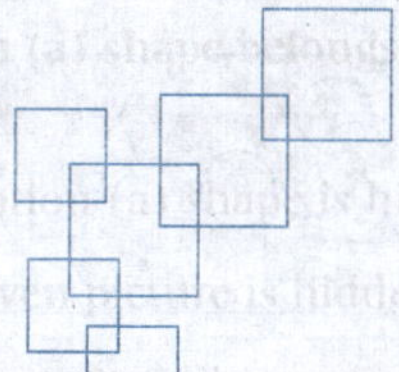

(a) 2 (b) 4
(c) 6 (d) 8

11. How many triangles does the below figure have?

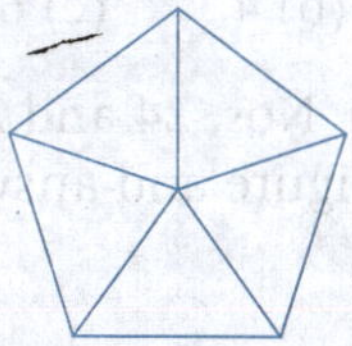

(a) 6 (b) 12
(c) 7 (d) 5

12. There are _____ triangles in the below figure.

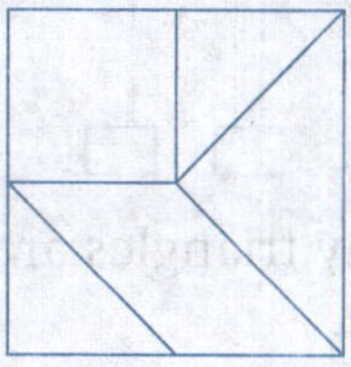

(a) 3 (b) 4
(c) 5 (d) 6

13. How many triangles present in the given figure?

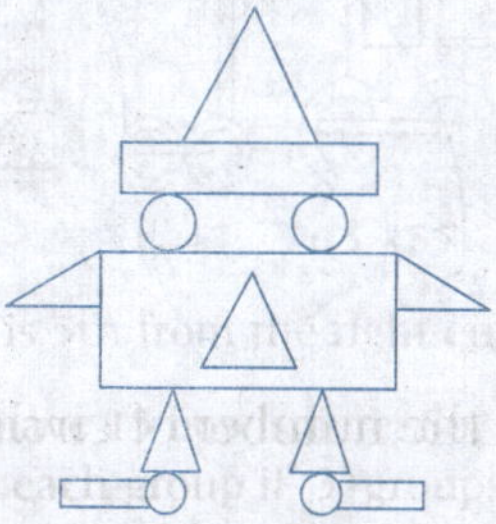

(a) 4 (b) 6
(c) 8 (d) 10

14. How many triangles are present in the figure?

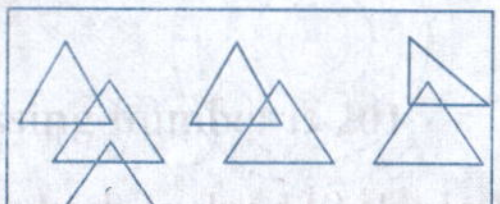

(a) 5 (b) 11
(c) 15 (d) 20

15. Count the number of circles in the following figure.

(a) 5 (b) 4
(c) 6 (d) 8

16. Count the number of circles in the below figure

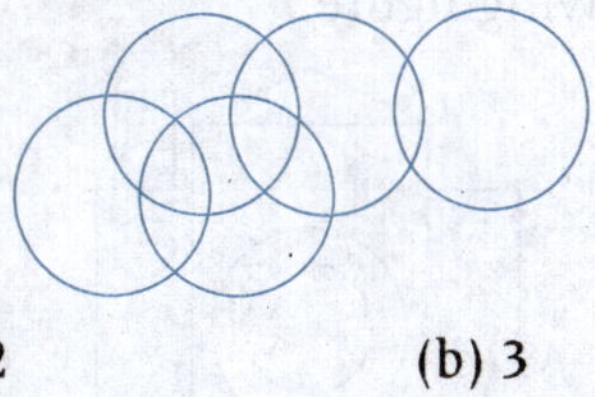

(a) 2 (b) 3
(c) 4 (d) 5

17. Marie drew a figure as shown below

Count the number of circles in the figure.

(a) 5 (b) 7 (c) 3 (d) 9

18. How many circles are present in the figure?

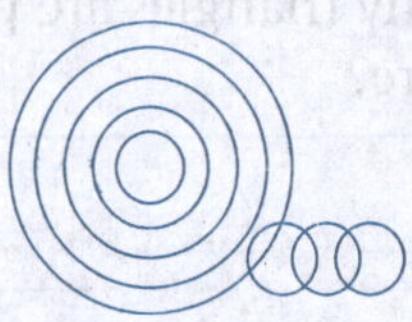

(a) 7 (b) 8 (c) 9 (d) 10

19. Brane has some parts of cardboard. He joins these parts to form a square. Count the number of card boards having triangular (△) shape.

(a) 4 (b) 8 (c) 6 (d) 9

20. There are ___ rectangles in the following figure.

(a) 6 (b) 7 (c) 4 (d) 5

21. There are ___ triangles and ___ circles in the below figure.

(a) 2, 4 (b) 4, 2 (c) 3, 5 (d) 4, 1

Directions (Q. Nos. 22 and 23) Observe the following figure to answer the given questions.

22. How many circles are present in the figure?

(a) 1 (b) 2 (c) 3 (d) 5

23. How many more triangles are there than the squares in the figure?

(a) 2 (b) 4 (c) 6 (d) 8

Directions (Q. Nos. 24 and 25) Observe the following figure and answer the given questions.

24. How many triangles are present in the figure.

(a) 1 (b) 2 (c) 3 (d) 4

25. Find the total number of circles.

(a) 5 (b) 6 (c) 7 (d) 8

Chapter 09

Position and Comparison Test

'Position and Comparison Test' means to find out the position of a person or an object in a row or queue.

Directions (Ex. Nos. 1 and 2) Observe the given figure carefully and answer the following questions.

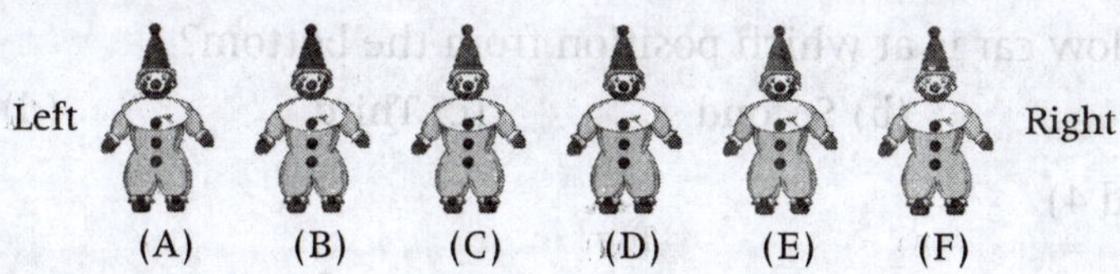

EXAMPLE 1 Which joker is third from the left end?

(a) B (b) A (c) D (d) C

EXAMPLE 2 Which joker is second from the right end?

(a) F (b) D (c) E (d) B

Sol. (Ex. Nos. 1 and 2)

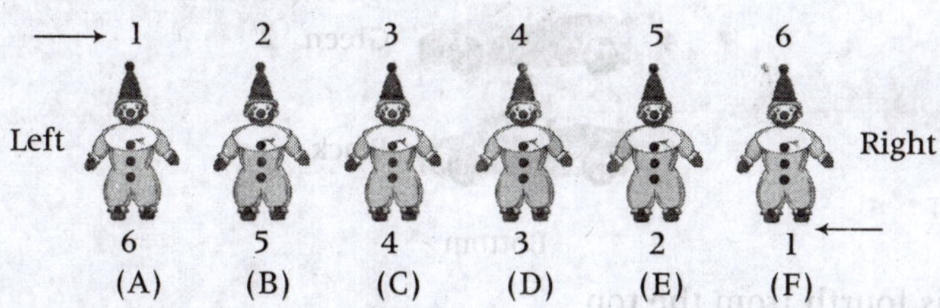

1. (d) Joker C is third from the left end.
Hence, option (d) is correct.

2. (c) Joker E is second from the right end.
Hence, option (c) is correct.

Directions (Ex. Nos. 3 and 4) Observe the following figures carefully and answer the questions given below.

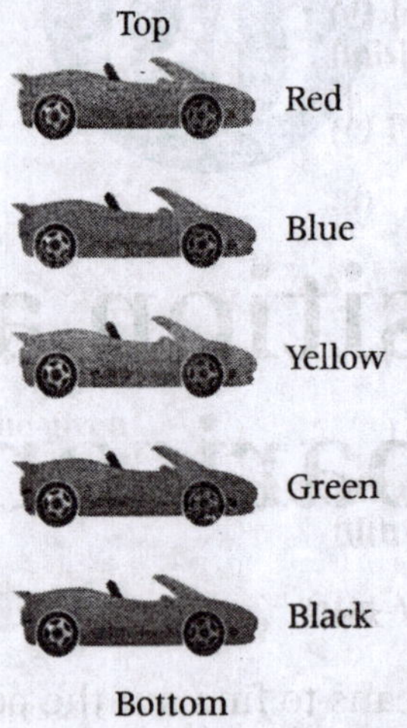

EXAMPLE 3 Which car is fourth from the top?

(a) Red (b) Blue (c) Yellow (d) Green

EXAMPLE 4 Yellow car is at which position from the bottom?

(a) First (b) Second (c) Third (d) Fourth

Sol. (Ex. Nos. 3 and 4)

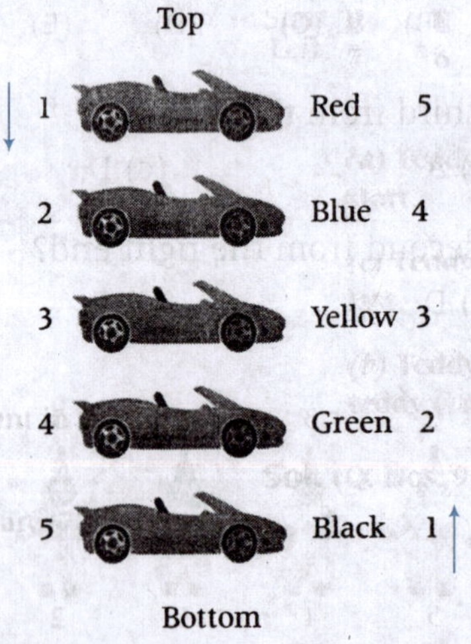

3. (d) Green car is fourth from the top.
Hence, option (d) is correct.

4. (c) Yellow car is at the third position from the bottom.
Hence, option (c) is correct.

Let's Practice

Directions (Q. Nos. 1-3) Observe the given figure carefully and answer the questions that follow.

1. Who is at the first position from right end?
   (a) Tim (b) Brane
   (c) Flora (d) Paul

2. Who is at the last position from the finishing line?
   (a) Joy (b) Brane
   (c) Paul (d) Tim

3. Who is at the third position from left end?
   (a) Tim (b) Flora
   (c) Paul (d) Brane

Directions (Q. Nos. 4 and 5) Observe the given figure carefully and answer the questions below.

4. If the ice-cream is removed from the arrangement shown above, then which item is fifth from the left end?
   (a) S (b) R
   (c) Q (d) U

5. If the lamp and the bottle interchange their positions, then which of the element will be second to the right of bottle?
   (a) S (b) T (c) R (d) P

Directions (Q. Nos. 6-8) Observe the given figure carefully and answer the questions that follow.

6. Teddy____ is at the fourth position from the start.
   (a) C (b) G
   (c) A (d) D

7. Teddy ____ is at the fifth position from the last.
   (a) C (b) G
   (c) A (d) E

8. Teddy ____ is to the immediate right of the third teddy.
   (a) G (b) C (c) A (d) D

Directions (Q. Nos. 9-11) Observe the given figure carefully and answer the questions given below.

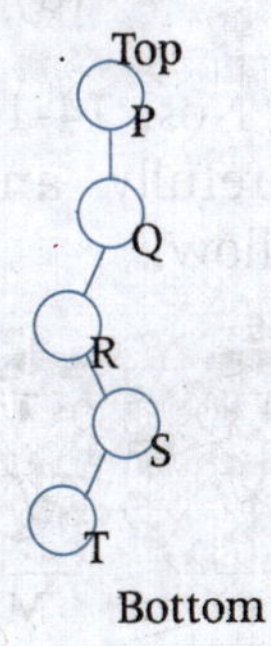

9. Which bead is fourth from the bottom?
(a) P (b) Q
(c) R (d) S

10. Which bead is at the middle position?
(a) P (b) Q
(c) R (d) S

11. Bead T is at the ___ position from the top?
(a) Fourth (b) Fifth
(c) Third (d) Second

Directions (Q. Nos. 12 and 13) Observe the given figure carefully and answer the questions below.

12. Which child is sixth from right?
(a) John (b) Lina
(c) Ray (d) Marie

13. Which child is third from the left?
(a) Julia (b) John
(c) Ray (d) Marie

Directions (Q. Nos. 14-16) Observe the given figure carefully and answer the questions that follow.

14. Which pilot is third to the left of pilot X1?
(a) P1 (b) J1
(c) M1 (d) B1

15. Pilot _____ is fourth to the right of first pilot from the left.
(a) Q1 (b) U1
(c) M1 (d) K1

16. Pilot _____ is third from the right end.
(a) U1 (b) K1
(c) P1 (d) X1

Directions (Q. Nos. 17-19) Observe the given figure carefully and answer the questions that follow.

17. Which cat is third to the left of rat R4?
(a) C1 (b) C2
(c) C3 (d) C4

18. If cat 1 and rat 3 interchange their positions, then _____ is third from the right end.
(a) R2 (b) C1
(c) R3 (d) C2

19. If we remove all the rats, then which of the following cat is immediate left of Cat 3?

(a) C1 (b) C2 (c) C3 (d) C4

Directions (Q. Nos. 20 and 21) Some boys are standing in a line, you have to observe the queue carefully and answer the questions that follow.

20. Which boy is sixth from the left end?

(a) P5 (b) J4 (c) P3 (d) J6

21. If P3 and J6 interchange their positions, then which boy will be third from the left of P3?

(a) P1 (b) J7 (c) J4 (d) P4

Directions (Q. Nos. 22 and 23) Some hats are putting in a line, you have to observe the queue carefully and answer the questions that follow.

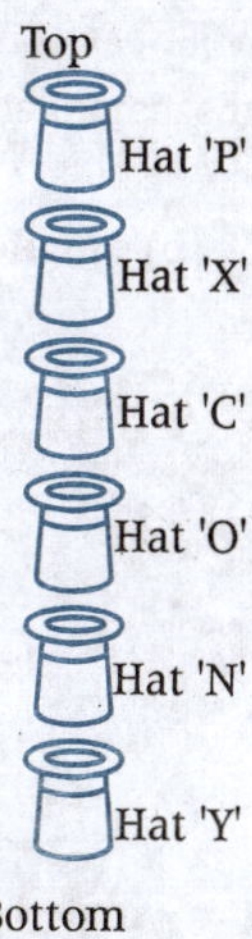

22. Which hat is fifth from the top?

(a) N (b) O
(c) Y (d) X

23. How many hats between 'Hat O' and 'Hat P'?

(a) 1 (b) 2
(c) 3 (d) 4

24. What is the name of the duck which is in middle of the arrangement?

Aiki Biki Ciki Diki Eiki

(a) Eiki (b) Biki
(c) Ciki (d) Aiki

25. If the rose is removed from the arrangement shown below, then which flower/fruit is sixth from the right end?

(a) Orange (b) Lotus
(c) Mango (d) Apple

26. Study the given picture carefully.

Which letter is fourth to the left of the third letter from the right end?

(a) X (b) Q (c) M (d) V

27. Study the given picture carefully.

Find the difference between the numbers which is third from the right and third from the left?

(a) 10 (b) 12 (c) 14 (d) 20

28. Observe the given figure carefully.

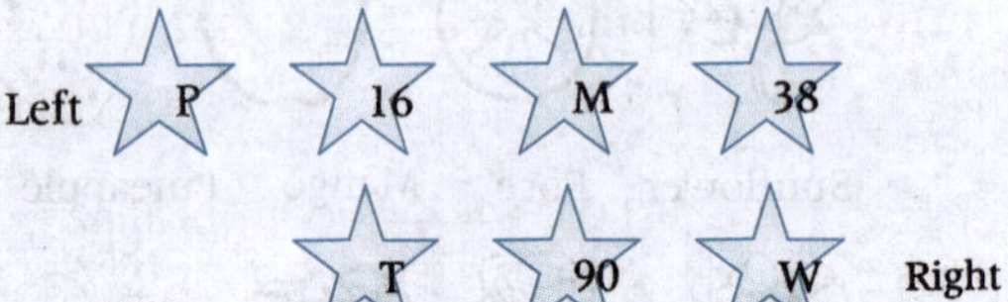

Which of the following star is middle of the arrangement?

(a) 38 (b) M
(c) T (d) 90

29. Some children are standing in a line

If R and U interchange their positions, then which child will be sixth from the right?

(a) Q
(b) S
(c) T
(d) U

30. _____ stairs are there between 5th stair and 12th stair ?

(a) 8
(b) 7
(c) 6
(d) 5

PRACTICE SETS 1-2

PRACTICE SET 01

1. Identify the figure which will complete the given figure series.

(a)  (b)  (c)  (d) 

2. Three out of four figures form a group. Identify the figure that does not fit into the group.

(a)  (b) 

(c)  (d) 

3. Which of the following figures will complete the figure (X)?

(X)

(a)  (b) 

(c)  (d) 

4. Which pattern completes the second pair in the same way as first pair?

(a)  (b) 

(c)  (d) 

5. Choose the figure which is different from others.

(a)  (b)  (c)  (d) 

6. What comes next in the following series?

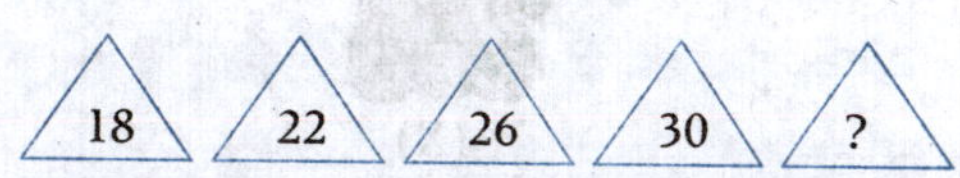

(a) 34 (b) 38 (c) 28 (d) 40

7. Complete the second pair in the same way as first pair.

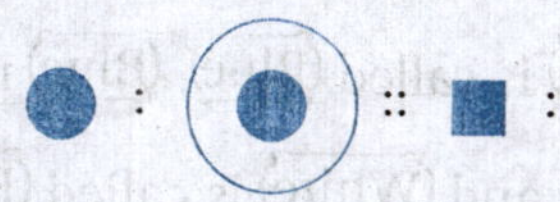

(a)  (b)  (c)  (d) 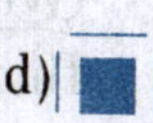

8. Find the missing number.

(a) 14 (b) 54 (c) 90 (d) 60

9. How many groups of 4 candies can be formed from given candies?

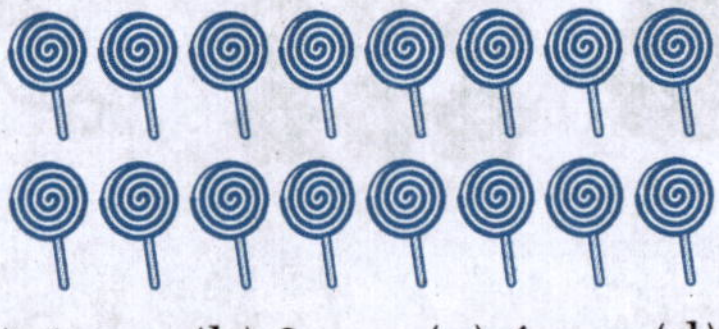

(a) 6 (b) 2 (c) 4 (d) 8

10. Which shape or pattern belongs to the group of shapes given?

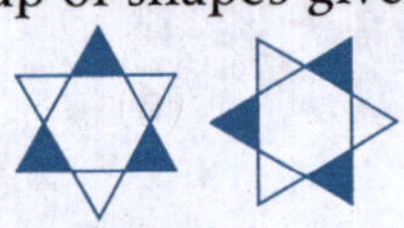

(a)  (b)  (c)  (d) 

11. Which of the following figure is hidden in the given figure(X)?

(X)

(a) (b) (c) (d)

12. If (Red) is called (Blue), (Blue) is called (White) and (White) is called (Pink), then what is the colour of milk?

(a) Pink (b) Red (c) Blue (d) White

13. Count the number of circles in the given figure.

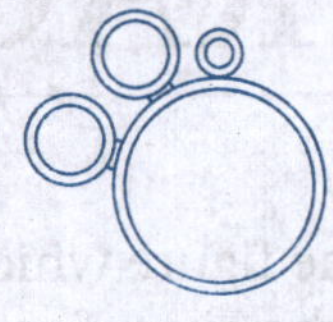

(a) 4 (b) 12 (c) 8 (d) 10

14. Observe the given figure carefully and answer the question given below.

Left  Right

(D) (P) (K) (J) (A) (C) (M) (L)

Which monkey is sixth from the right end?

(a) K (b) D (c) A (d) J

15. If 970 is coded as 079, then find the code of 816 ?

(a) 861 (b) 168 (c) 186 (d) 618

16. As PMJC is related to 151292, then in the same way CQXI is related to?

(a) 213268 (b) 221368
(c) 216238 (d) 216228

17. Identify the odd group of letters?

RUX	JMP	CFJ	XAD
(a)	(b)	(c)	(d)

18. Find the next letters in the given series?

(a) ZX (b) VZ
(c) AV (d) UX

19. If 'SIGNAL' is coded as 'ISNGLA', then how word 'SUMMER' is coded as?

(a) USMMRE (b) USMRME
(c) MMREUS (d) SREUMM

20. Complete the given alphabetical series.

J, KK, LLL, MMMM, NNNNN, ?

(a) OOOOO (b) PPPP
(c) QQQ (d) OOOOOO

21. Find odd one out.

4216	7133	6151	4324
(a)	(b)	(c)	(d)

22. Find the figure pattern of the given figure (X).

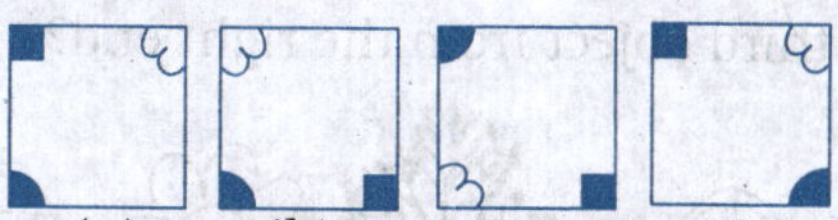

(a) (b) (c) (d)

23. If 'Mango' is called 'Blue', 'Blue' is called 'Yellow', 'Yellow is called Apple' and 'Apple is called red'. Then what is the colour of 'Mango'?

(a) Blue (b) Yellow (c) Apple (d) Red

24. Which shape or pattern belongs to the group of shapes given below?

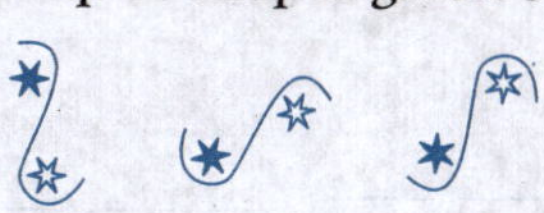

(a)  (b) 

(c)  (d) 

25. Observe the given picture carefully.

Which shape is hidden in given the picture?

(a) (b) (c) (d)

26. Find the total number of circles in the given figure.

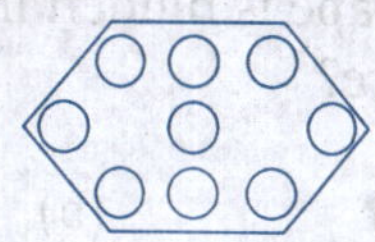

(a) 7 (b) 8 (c) 9 (d) 10

27. Which shape or pattern belongs to the group of shapes given below?

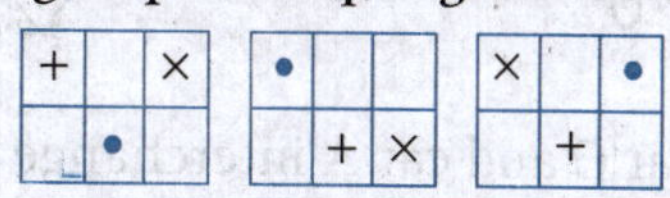

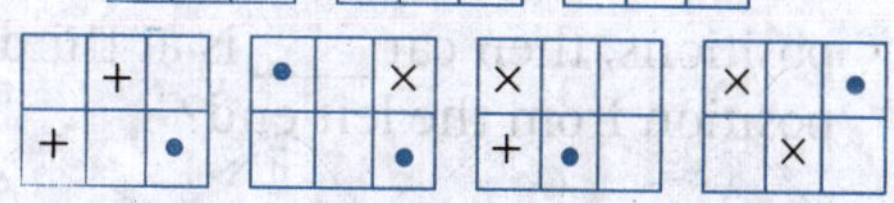

(a) (b) (c) (d)

How many triangles are there in the pattern?

(a) 4 (b) 5 (c) 6 (d) 7

Directions (Q. Nos. 29 and 30) Observe the picture carefully and answer the questions based on it.

29. In which part of the picture is the shape  hidden?

(a) 1 (b) 2 (c) 3 (d) 4

30. Which shape is hidden in part '3' of the picture?

(a)  (b) 

(c)  (d) 

31. If car C and car A interchange their positions, then car ____ is at third position from the left end?

Car C Car E Car A Car G

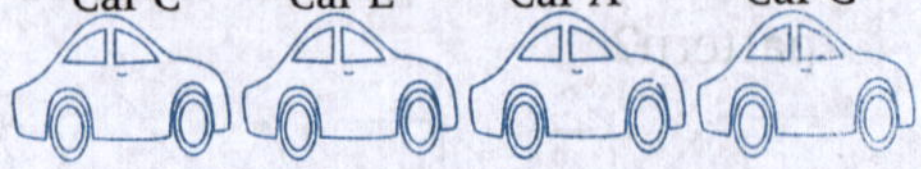

Car F Car B Car D Car M

(a) Car E (b) Car B (c) Car C (d) Car F

32. How many trees are required, if we need to form '6' groups of '2' trees using given trees?

(a) 1 (b) 2 (c) 3 (d) 4

33. Which of the following figure has has exactly three squares?

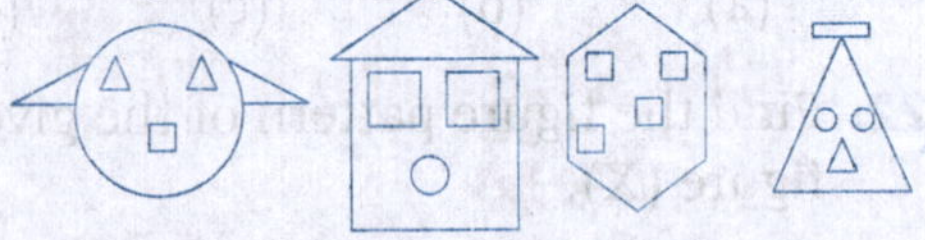

(a) (b) (c) (d)

34. If the 'Kite' is removed from the arrangement shown below, then which object is second to the left of third object from the right end?

(a) Doll (b) Flower (c) Car (d) Tree

35. Find the missing term on the train bogie.

(a) 792 (b) 972 (c) 297 (d) 793

PRACTICE SET 02

1. If (CAT) is coded as (TAC), then find the code for (RAT).
(a) TRA (b) TAR
(c) ATR (d) RTA

2. Which of the following figures will complete the figure (X)?

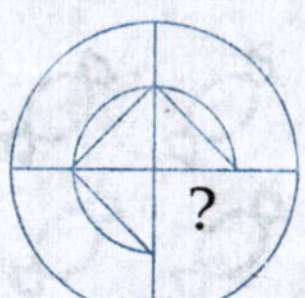
(X)

(a)  (b) 
(c) 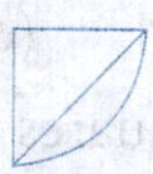 (d) 

3. Which is the odd one out?

(a)  (b) 
(c)  (d) 

4. Complete the second pair in the same way as first pair.

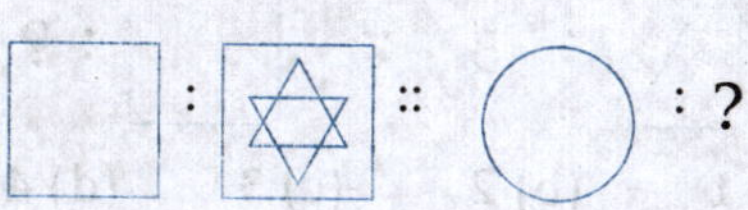

(a)  (b) 
(c) 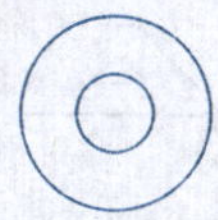 (d) 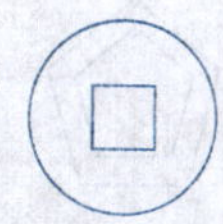

5. Identify the figure which will complete the given figure series.

(a)  (b) 
(c)  (d) 

6. If  Tailor is called  Doctor,  Doctor is called  Barber and  Barber is called  Postman, then who cuts our hair?
(a) Tailor
(b) Postman
(c) Doctor
(d) Barber

7. Which shape or pattern belongs to the given group?

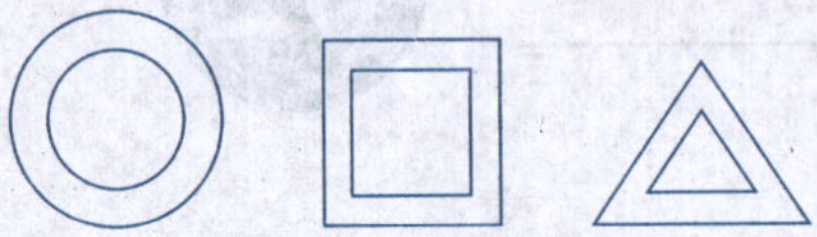

(a) 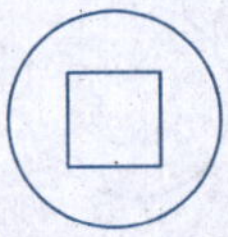 (b) 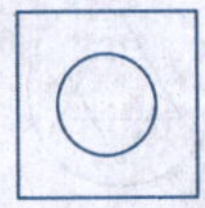

(c)  (d) 

8. Choose the figure which is different from others.

(a)  (b) 

(c)  (d) 

9. How many caps will be there in pattern 4?

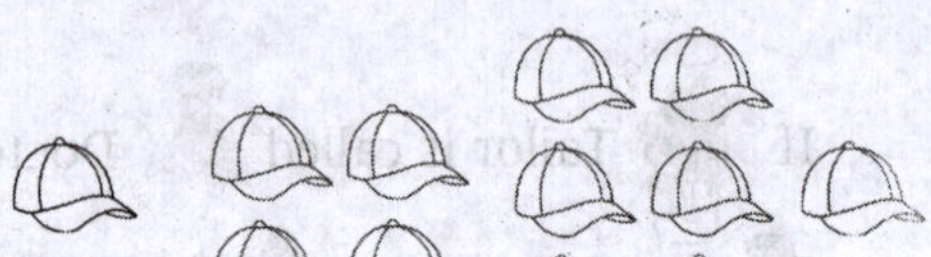

Pattern 1 Pattern 2 Pattern 3

(a) 12 (b) 10 (c) 8 (d) 9

10. If the star is removed from the arrangement shown below, then which is the sixth item from the left end?

(a)  (b) 

(c)  (d) 

11. Complete the number pattern.

(25) (31) (37) (43) (49) (?)

(a) 50 (b) 55 (c) 65 (d) 52

12. How many toffees are required, if we need to form 4 groups of 5 toffees using given toffees?

(a) 1 (b) 2 (c) 3 (d) 4

13. Count the number of squares in the following figure.

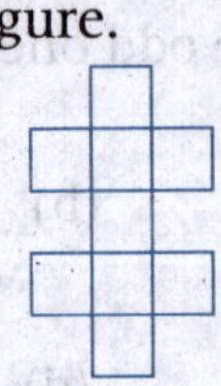

(a) 10 (b) 8 (c) 9 (d) 11

14. Complete the second pair in the same way as first pair.

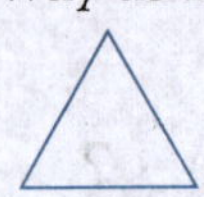 : 3 :: 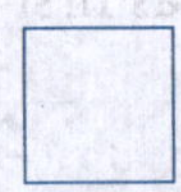 : ?

(a) 1 (b) 2 (c) 3 (d) 4

15. Which of the following shape is hidden in the given figure (X)?

(X)

(a)  (b) 

(c)  (d) 

16. As 'DMJP' is related to 'GPMS' in the same way ZXBN is related to?

(a) AECQ (b) CAEQ

(c) ACEQ (d) ECQA

17. Identify the odd group of numbers.

21	49	36	63
(a)	(b)	(c)	(d)

18. Find the missing number in the question given below, there is a relationship between the numbers in the first and second rows.

First Row : 8 16 24 32

Second Row : 5 10 ? 20

(a) 15 (b) 25

(c) 35 (d) 30

19. If 'PAYAL' is coded as 'QBZBM', then how word 'SWITCH' is coded as?

(a) TJXUDI (b) TXUJID

(c) TXJUDI (d) DXUJIT

20. Complete the given alphabetical series.

M, NO, PQR, STUV, ?

(a) WXYZA

(b) WYZAX

(c) UYZAX

(d) AZXTS

21. Find odd one out.

718	9514	628	318
(a)	(b)	(c)	(d)

22. Complete the given figure (X).

(a)  (b)  (c)  (d) 

23. If SIYA is coded as 1@#8 and PAPA is coded as 3838, then how PIYA is coded as?

(a) @#83 (b) 3@#8

(c) 8@#3 (d) @#38

24. In which group the given shape belongs.

Shape

P Q R

(a) P only (b) Q only

(c) Both P, Q (d) P, Q and R

25. Observe the given picture carefully.

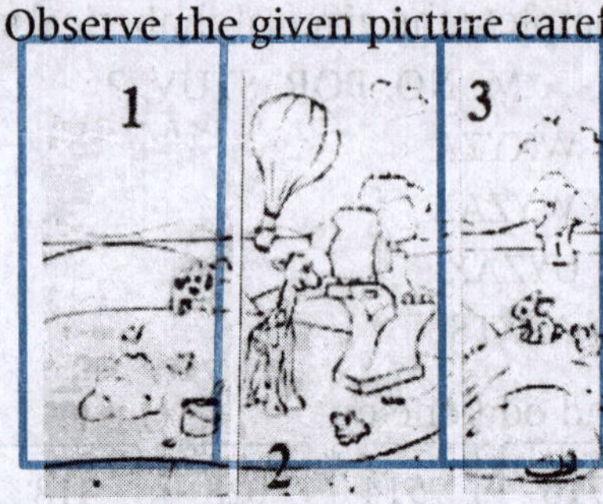

In which part of the picture is the shape  hidden?

(a) 1 (b) 3
(c) 2 (d) None of these

26. Find the total number of triangles.

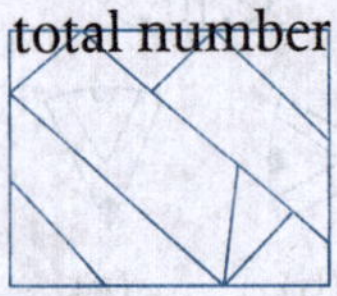

(a) 2 (b) 3
(c) 4 (d) 5

27. Which shape or pattern belongs to the group of shapes given below?

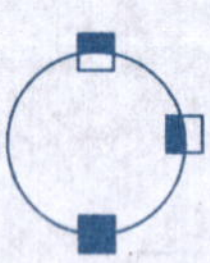
(a)

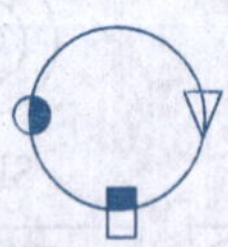
(b)

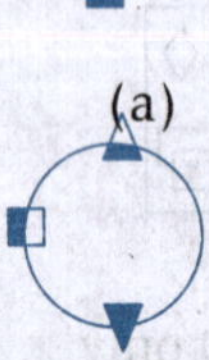
(c)

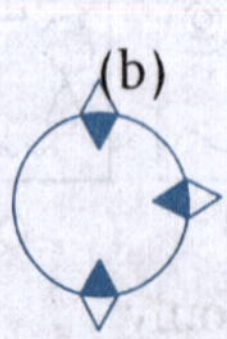
(d)

Directions (Q. Nos. 28 and 29) Observe the picture carefully and answer the questions based on it.

28. Which shape is hidden in the part '3' of the picture?

 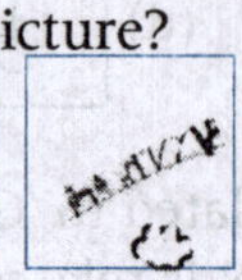  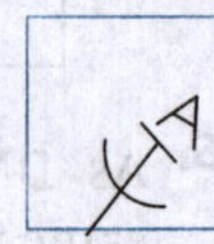

(a) (b) (c) (d)

29. In which part of the picture is the shape  hidden?

(a) 1 (b) 2
(c) 3 (d) 4

30. How many circles are present in the given shape?

(a) 6 (b) 7
(c) 8 (d) 9

31. Which of the following kid is 5th from the right end?

(a) E1 (b) E2 (c) J1 (d) J2

32. How many bowls are there in each group, if 3 groups of equal number of bowls are formed from given bowls?

(a) 4 (b) 5 (c) 6 (d) 7

33. There are .... triangles and squares respectively in the given figure?

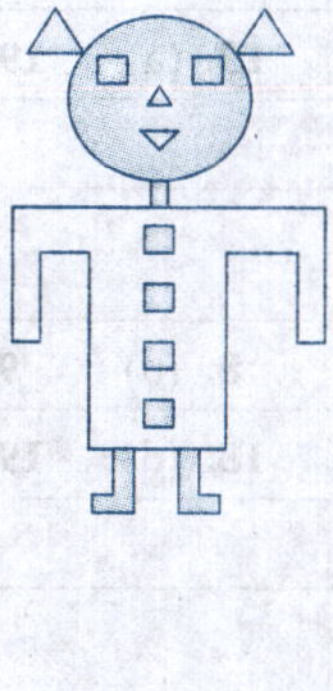

(a) 3, 6
(b) 4, 6
(c) 6, 3
(d) 4, 2

34. Find the missing number in the following series?

181 186 191 196 ?

(a) 205
(b) 201
(c) 200
(d) 198

35. If we removed Monu who is playing basketball, then which of the following kid is third to the left of the third kid from the right end?

(a) Tiya
(b) Abhini
(c) Zack
(d) Diki

ANSWERS

1. Matching Pairs

1. (a)	**2.** (d)	**3.** (a)	**4.** (c)	**5.** (d)	**6.** (d)	**7.** (b)	**8.** (c)	**9.** (c)	**10.** (c)
11. (b)	**12.** (a)	**13.** (a)	**14.** (b)	**15.** (b)	**16.** (c)	**17.** (a)	**18.** (c)	**19.** (c)	**20.** (d)
21. (a)	**22.** (a)	**23.** (a)	**24.** (b)	**25.** (a)	**26.** (b)	**27.** (d)	**28.** (b)	**29.** (a)	**30.** (c)

2. Odd One Out

1. (a)	**2.** (c)	**3.** (c)	**4.** (a)	**5.** (c)	**6.** (c)	**7.** (d)	**8.** (c)	**9.** (d)	**10.** (b)
11. (b)	**12.** (c)	**13.** (c)	**14.** (d)	**15.** (d)	**16.** (d)	**17.** (d)	**18.** (d)	**19.** (b)	**20.** (b)
21. (c)	**22.** (c)	**23.** (c)	**24.** (c)	**25.** (d)	**26.** (b)				

3. What Comes Next?

1. (b)	**2.** (c)	**3.** (c)	**4.** (a)	**5.** (c)	**6.** (d)	**7.** (b)	**8.** (d)	**9.** (a)	**10.** (c)
11. (d)	**12.** (a)	**13.** (b)	**14.** (b)	**15.** (a)	**16.** (a)	**17.** (d)	**18.** (c)	**19.** (b)	**20.** (d)
21. (b)	**22.** (b)	**23.** (b)	**24.** (b)	**25.** (c)	**26.** (b)				

4. Coding-Decoding

1. (b)	**2.** (b)	**3.** (d)	**4.** (c)	**5.** (a)	**6.** (b)	**7.** (b)	**8.** (a)	**9.** (b)	**10.** (d)
11. (b)	**12.** (a)	**13.** (d)	**14.** (a)	**15.** (b)	**16.** (b)	**17.** (a)	**18.** (a)	**19.** (c)	**20.** (d)
21. (c)									

5. Complete the Figure

1. (b)	**2.** (d)	**3.** (d)	**4.** (d)	**5.** (c)	**6.** (a)	**7.** (c)	**8.** (a)	**9.** (c)	**10.** (d)
11. (a)	**12.** (d)	**13.** (d)	**14.** (a)	**15.** (a)	**16.** (a)	**17.** (c)	**18.** (a)	**19.** (b)	**20.** (c)
21. (b)	**22.** (d)	**23.** (d)	**24.** (b)	**25.** (b)					

6. Find Similar Figure and Grouping of Figures

1. (c)	**2.** (c)	**3.** (d)	**4.** (a)	**5.** (c)	**6.** (d)	**7.** (a)	**8.** (b)	**9.** (c)	**10.** (d)
11. (c)	**12.** (b)	**13.** (a)	**14.** (c)	**15.** (b)	**16.** (d)	**17.** (c)	**18.** (d)	**19.** (c)	**20.** (d)
21. (d)	**22.** (a)	**23.** (b)	**24.** (a)	**25.** (c)					

7. Hidden Figures

1. (c)	**2.** (d)	**3.** (b)	**4.** (a)	**5.** (c)	**6.** (b)	**7.** (b)	**8.** (c)	**9.** (c)	**10.** (a)
11. (d)	**12.** (c)	**13.** (c)	**14.** (d)	**15.** (b)	**16.** (c)	**17.** (d)	**18.** (a)	**19.** (d)	**20.** (a)
21. (c)	**22.** (b)	**23.** (b)	**24.** (a)	**25.** (d)	**26.** (a)	**27.** (d)			

8. Counting of Figures

1. (b)	**2.** (d)	**3.** (d)	**4.** (c)	**5.** (c)	**6.** (a)	**7.** (c)	**8.** (d)	**9.** (c)	**10.** (c)
11. (d)	**12.** (a)	**13.** (b)	**14.** (b)	**15.** (a)	**16.** (d)	**17.** (b)	**18.** (b)	**19.** (a)	**20.** (d)
21. (a)	**22.** (d)	**23.** (a)	**24.** (b)	**25.** (c)					

9. Position and Comparison Test

1. (d)	**2.** (a)	**3.** (b)	**4.** (d)	**5.** (a)	**6.** (a)	**7.** (c)	**8.** (b)	**9.** (b)	**10.** (c)
11. (b)	**12.** (c)	**13.** (b)	**14.** (c)	**15.** (b)	**16.** (d)	**17.** (b)	**18.** (b)	**19.** (b)	**20.** (c)
21. (d)	**22.** (a)	**23.** (b)	**24.** (c)	**25.** (a)	**26.** (b)	**27.** (c)	**28.** (a)	**29.** (d)	**30.** (c)

Practice Set 1

1. (b)	**2.** (d)	**3.** (c)	**4.** (d)	**5.** (d)	**6.** (a)	**7.** (c)	**8.** (b)	**9.** (c)	**10.** (c)
11. (b)	**12.** (a)	**13.** (c)	**14.** (a)	**15.** (d)	**16.** (c)	**17.** (c)	**18.** (b)	**19.** (a)	**20.** (d)
21. (b)	**22.** (b)	**23.** (c)	**24.** (b)	**25.** (a)	**26.** (c)	**27.** (c)	**28.** (c)	**29.** (b)	**30.** (b)
31. (c)	**32.** (a)	**33.** (b)	**34.** (d)	**35.** (b)					

Practice Set 2

1. (b)	**2.** (d)	**3.** (b)	**4.** (a)	**5.** (c)	**6.** (b)	**7.** (c)	**8.** (a)	**9.** (b)	**10.** (a)
11. (b)	**12.** (a)	**13.** (c)	**14.** (d)	**15.** (b)	**16.** (b)	**17.** (c)	**18.** (a)	**19.** (c)	**20.** (a)
21. (d)	**22.** (d)	**23.** (b)	**24.** (c)	**25.** (b)	**26.** (d)	**27.** (a)	**28.** (a)	**29.** (a)	**30.** (c)
31. (a)	**32.** (b)	**33.** (b)	**34.** (b)	**35.** (c)					

Hints & Solutions

1. Matching Pairs

1. *(a)* The shape given in first figure is covered by the similar shape having dotted lines out side.

   So, figure in option (a) will complete the second pair.

2. *(d)* The number of elements is increased by two to get the second figure.

   So, figure in option (d) will complete the second pair.

3. *(a)* The shaded portion is taken forward to get the second figure.

   So, figure in option (a) will complete the second pair.

4. *(c)* The four parts of the square get separated from figure first to second.

   So, figure in option (c) will complete the second pair.

5. *(d)* First figure is flipped down to get the second figure.

   So, figure in option (d) will complete the second pair.

6. *(d)* From figure first to third, the outer lines of the shape get dotted.

   So, figure in option (d) must be the figure 4.

7. *(b)* As, a policeman travels in the police car, similarly an astronaut travels in rocket.

   So, figure in option (b) will complete the second pair.

8. *(c)* In first pair, the two dogs are sitting in first figure and running in second figure. Similarly, in second pair the two boys are sitting in first figure and will run in second figure.

   So, figure in option (c) will complete the second pair.

9. *(c)* As, we keep food in oven, similarly we keep post card or letter in post box.

   So, figure in option (c) will complete the second pair.

10. *(c)* Arrows appear facing outside at the corner of the shape, from figure first to second.

    So, figure in option (c) will complete the second pair.

11. *(b)* As, fish lives in the pond, similarly lion lives in the forest.

    Hence, option (b) is correct.

12. *(a)* As, we use bat to hit the ball. Similarly, we use badminton bat to hit the shuttle.

13. *(a)* First figure is flipped down to get the second figure.

    So, figure in option (a) will complete the second pair.

14. *(b)* As, aeroplane is fly in the sky. Similarly, train runs always on railway track.

    So, figure (b) will complete the second pair.

15. *(b)* As, $₹100 \times 2 = ₹200$

    Similarly, $₹500 \times 2 = ₹1000$

    So, the note of ₹ 1000 in option (b) will complete the second pair.

16. *(c)* As, $3 + 4 = 7$

    Similarly, $2 + 4 = 6$

    So, number in option (c) will complete the second pair.

17. *(a)* As, $1 + 8 = 9$, similarly, $1 + 7 = 8$

    So, number in option (a) will complete the second pair.

18. *(c)* As, $2 \times 4 = 8$

    Similarly, $5 \times 4 = \boxed{20}$

    So, number in option (c) will complete the second pair.

19. *(c)* As, $1 + 8 = 9$

    Similarly, $3 + 7 = 10$

    So, number in option (c) will complete the second pair.

20. *(d)* As,

3 0 3
+1 +2
4 [0] 5

Similarly,

7 0 7
+1 +2
8 [0] 9

So, number in option (d) will complete the second pair.

21. *(a)* As,

4 6 8
+3 +3 −1
7 9 7

Similarly,

6 9 5
+3 +3 −1
9 12 4

So, the number in option (a) will complete the second pair.

22. *(a)* Consecutive letters given in each pairs.
So, letter in option (a) will complete the second pair.

23. *(a)* There are two letters between the letters of first pair.
So, letter in option (a) will complete the second pair.

24. *(b)* As, Pp $\xrightarrow{+1}$ Qq
Similarly, Zz $\xrightarrow{+1}$ Aa
So, the letters in option (b) will be the correct matching pair.

25. *(a)* As, J $\xrightarrow[\text{Letter}]{\text{Reverse}}$ Q
Similarly, M $\xrightarrow[\text{Letter}]{\text{Reverse}}$ [N]
So, the letter in option (a) will complete the second pair.

26. *(b)* As, HIJK $\xrightarrow[\text{LMNO}]{+5}$ PQRS
Similarly, XYZA $\xrightarrow[\text{BCDE}]{+5}$ FGHI
So, the group of letters given in option (b) will complete the second pair.

27. *(d)* As, C $\xrightarrow{+2}$ e $\xrightarrow{+2}$ GhI ⟶ D f (+1, +1)
Similarly, M $\xrightarrow{+2}$ o $\xrightarrow{+2}$ Q r S ⟶ N p (+1, +1)
So, the letters in option (d) will complete the second pair.

28. *(b)* As, dog bark, similarly the cat mew.
So, word in option (b) will complete the second pair.

29. *(a)* As, for taking the education we go to 'School'. In the same way for doing 'prayer' we go to the 'Church'.

30. *(c)* As, MANGO have 5 letters so, $5^2 = 25$
Similarly, LITCHI have 6 letters so, $6^2 = 36$
So, the number in option (c) will complete the second pair.

2. Odd One Out

1. *(a)* Except mango all others are flower, while mango is fruit. So, option figure (a) is different from others.

2. *(c)* Pea in figure (c) is closed while in others it is open.
So, option figure (c) is different from others.

3. *(c)* Bug in figure (c) is facing in different direction while all others are facing in same direction.
So, option figure (c) is odd one out.

4. *(a)* Except option (a), in all other options different birds are given.
So, option figure (a) is odd one out.

5. *(c)* Figure (c) shows picture of a bat, while all others show different balls.
So, option figure (c) is odd figure.

6. *(c)* In all other figures except figure (c), both the lines are overlapping each other.
So, option figure (c) is odd figure.

7. *(d)* In all the figures except (d), the number of sides is equal to the number of circles, But in option figure (d), the number of sides is 6 and the number of circles is 5. So option figure (d) is odd figure.

8. *(c)* Arrow in figure (c) is different, while the arrows in all other figures are same. So, figure (c) is odd figure.

9. *(d)* In all the figures except figure (d), two same shapes are overlapping each other. So , option figure (d) is odd figure.

10. *(b)* In figure (b), three circles and one square are given, while in all others two circles and two squares are given. So, option figure (b) is different from others.

11. *(b)* Except option (b), all the flowers have five petals.

12. *(c)* Except option figure (c), all the given objects are the parts of computer.

13. *(c)* Except option (c), the circles are present on the corner of square and other is adjacent of corner. While in option (c) both circles are present on mid of line of square.

14. *(d)* Except option (d) all triangles have 3 stars while option (d) have 4 stars.

15. *(d)* Except mango 36, all mangoes are present in tree.

16. *(d)* Except 6, all others are odd numbers. So, option (d) is different from others.

17. *(d)* Except option (d), all others are consecutive numbers. So, option (d) is odd one.

18. *(d)* Except option (d) '19', all others are multiple of '4'.

19. *(b)* Except option (b) '100', all others have only one 'zero'.

20. *(b)* Except option (b) '2009', all others are even number years.

21. *(c)* Except option (d) '98', the sum of the two digits are '13', while $9 + 8 = 17 \neq 13$.

22. *(c)* Except option (c) '73', multiplication of all other digits are '16' while the multiplication of 73 will be $7 \times 3 = 21$.

23. *(c)* Except option (c) '6', all are prime numbers.

24. *(c)* Except option (c), all are multiple of '12'.

25. *(d)* Except option (d) 'S', the alphabetical place value of all letters are even. While, 'S' is on 19th place.

26. *(b)* Except option (b), all other letters are written in descending order. So, option (b) is odd one.

3. What Comes Next?

1. *(b)* Each figure repeats itself after every two figures. So, the next figure will be

2. *(c)* Each figure repeats itself after every three figures. So, the next figure will be

3. *(c)* In each step, the engine moves one step forward. So, the next figure will be same as option figure (c).

4. *(a)* In each successive step an outer square is added. So, the next figure will be

There are 5 squares in the above figure.

5. *(c)* In each successive step the black circle shifts one position downward.

So, the missing figure will be

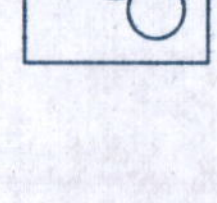

6. *(d)* Each time a circle is removed. So, there will be three circles in the next figure as shown below

7. *(b)* Each time the number of arrow heads increases by 1. So, the next figure will be

8. *(d)*  appears after every two .
So, the next figure will be

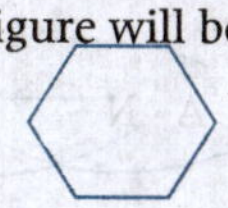

9. *(a)* Each shape repeats itself after every three figures. So, the next figure will be

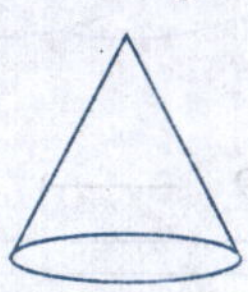

10. *(c)* Flowers are increases by one in the each step. So, the next figure will be shown is option figure (c).

11. *(d)* The pattern is as follows:
The pentagon is increase in each step by one.
So, the option figure (d) 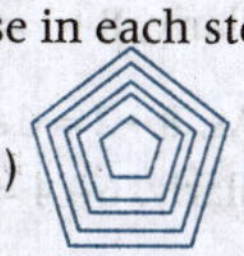 is our answer.

12. *(a)* The pattern is as follows:
In each step one arrow, one circle and one arrow faces opposite direction present respectively. So, option (a) arrow faces opposite direction to the given question figure arrow.
So, our answer is option (a) 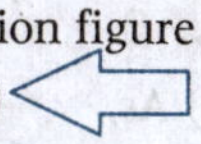.

13. *(b)* The given process is an eating a banana.
So, option (b) part will be the last step.

14. *(b)* When we start to draw a mango the last figure will be option (b) mango.

15. *(a)* Each number repeats itself after three numbers. So, the missing number will be 3.

16. *(a)* The pattern is as follows

$22 \xrightarrow{+3} 25 \xrightarrow{+3} 28 \xrightarrow{+3} 31 \xrightarrow{+3} 34$

So, the missing term will be 31.

17. *(d)* The pattern is as follows

$15 \xrightarrow{+10} 25 \xrightarrow{+15} 40 \xrightarrow{+20} 60 \xrightarrow{+25} 85$

So, the missing number will be 85.

18. *(c)* The pattern is as follows:

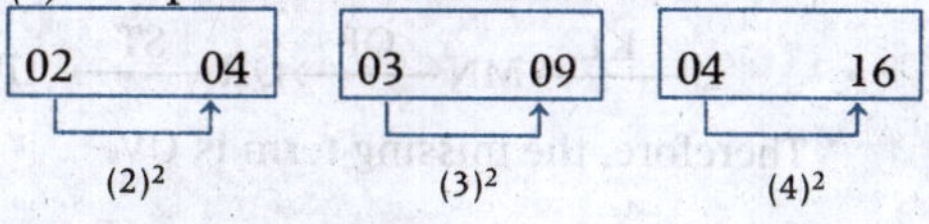

So, 16 is our answer.

19. *(b)* The pattern is as follows:
Here + 10 is added in each number

$41 \xrightarrow{+10} 51 \xrightarrow{+10} 61 \xrightarrow{+10} 71 \xrightarrow{+10} \boxed{81}$

So, the next number is 81.

20. *(d)* The pattern is as follows:

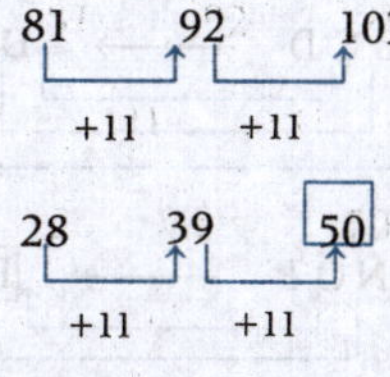

So, the next number is 50.

21. *(b)* The pattern is as follows:

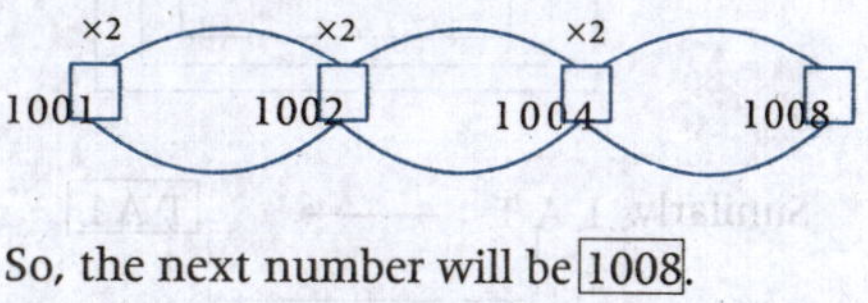

So, the next number will be $\boxed{1008}$.
Here, 100 is constant.

22. (b) The pattern is as follows :
As, $9 \times 5 = 45$
Similarly, $13 \times 7 = 91$
So, the next number will be 91.

23. (b) The pattern is as follows

XYZYUU | XYZYUU | XYZYUU | XY

So, the next letter will be Y.

24. (b) The pattern is as follows

BDCC | BDCC | BDCC | B

So, the next term will be B.

25. (c) The pattern is as follows

J —KL→ M —NO→ P —QR→ S —TU→ V —WX→ Y

So, the missing letter will be Y.

26. (b) The pattern will be

IJ —KL→ MN —OP→ QR —ST→ UV

Therefore, the missing term is UV.

4. Coding-Decoding

1. (b) As, X Z ⟶ Z X and T U ⟶ U T

Similarly, P Q ⟶ Q P

2. (b) As, B C D ⟶ D C B

Similarly, N O P ⟶ P O N

3. (d) As, D A R ⟶ R A D

Similarly, L A T ⟶ T A L

4. (c) As, P Q R —(+3)→ U V W

Similarly, I J K —(+3)→ N O P

5. (a) As, G I K —(reverse alphabetical value)→ T R P

Similarly, U W Y —(Reverse alphabetical Value)→ F D B

6. (b) As, M A N ⟶ M B O (+1)

Similarly, V A N ⟶ V B O (+1)

7. (b) As, 2 4 9 ⟶ 9 4 2

and 3 0 1 ⟶ 1 0 3

Similarly, 7 9 6 ⟶ 6 9 7

8. (a) As, $7 + 3 = 10$, and $7 + 1 = 8$
Similarly, $8 + 1 = 9$

9. (b) As, $8 - 2 = 6$ and $4 - 3 = 1$
Similarly, $6 - 4 = 2$

10. (d) As, 100 ⟶ 1 100 1
(100 is constant)
Similarly, 300 ⟶ 3 300 3
(300 is constant)

11. (b) As, 8 —(×20)→ 80 × 160 (×10)

Similarly, 4 →(×20) 40 × 80 (×10)

12. *(a)* As,

2002 ⟶ 0220

Similarly,

9009 ⟶ 0990

13. *(d)* The colour of grass is green but here green is called white.

So, the colour of grass is white.

14. *(a)* Sunday comes after Saturday but here Sunday is called Monday.

So, Monday comes after Saturday.

15. *(b)* The colour of mango is yellow but here mango is called orange.

So, the colour of orange is yellow.

16. *(b)* We cut the vegetable from knife and here knife is called vegetable itself.

17. *(a)* Our national flower is 'Lotus' and here 'Lotus' is called 'Rose'.

18. *(a)* A person sleeps on bed but here bed is called carpet.

So, a person sleeps on carpet.

19. *(c)* We write on notebook but here notebook is called pen.

So, we write on pen.

20. *(d)* As, Code for IN is → @#

So, P I N K ⟶ Q @ # L (+1, +1)

Similarly,

Code for D I N E ⟶ E @ # F (+1, +1)

21. *(c)* The code for GAIN from the given table is @1#p

5. Complete the Figure

1. *(b)* Figure in option (b) will complete the given pattern as shown below

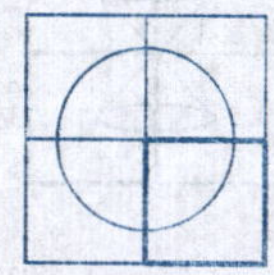

2. *(d)* Figure in option (d) will complete the given pattern as shown below

3. *(d)* Figure in option (d) will complete the given pattern as shown below

4. *(d)* Figure in option (d) will complete the given pattern as shown below

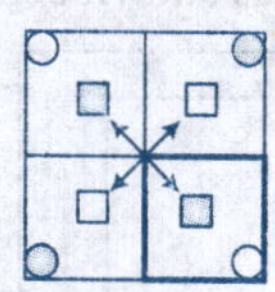

5. *(c)* Figure in option (c) will complete the given pattern as shown below

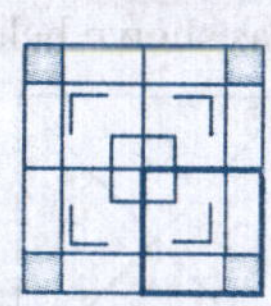

6. *(a)* Figure in option (a) will complete the given pattern as shown below

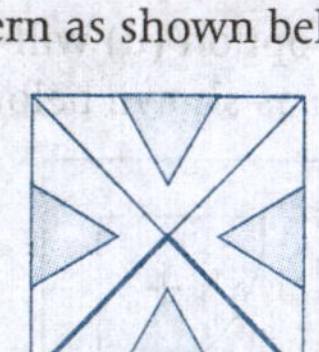

7. *(c)* Figure in option (c) will complete the given pattern as shown below

8. *(a)* Figure in option (a) will complete the given pattern as shown below

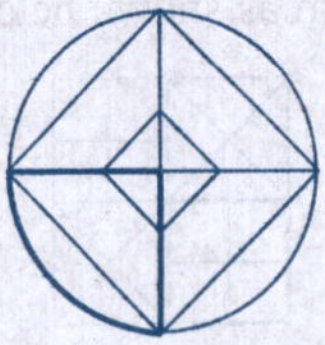

9. *(c)* Figure in option (c) will complete the given pattern as shown below.

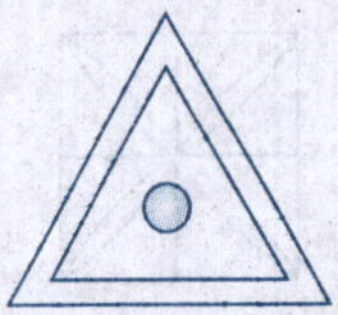

10. *(d)* Figure in option (d) will complete the given pattern as shown below.

11. *(a)* Figure in option (a) will complete the given pattern as shown below.

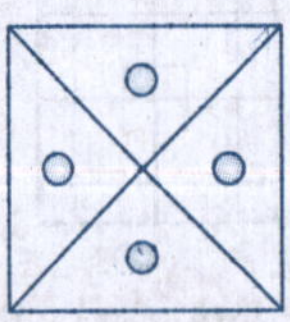

12. *(d)* Figure in option (d) will complete the given pattern as shown below.

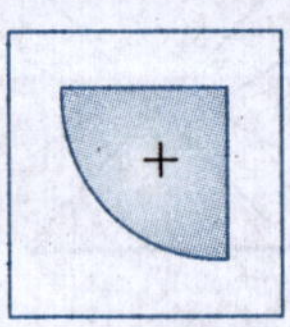

13. *(d)* Figure in option (d) will complete the given pattern as shown below.

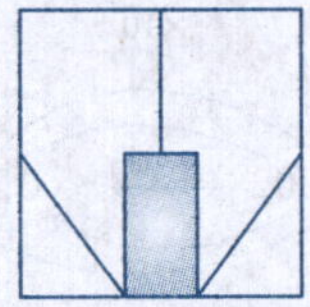

14. *(a)* Figure in option (a) will complete the given pattern as shown below.

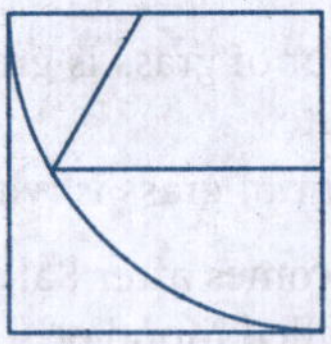

15. *(a)* Option figure (a) 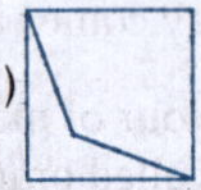 will complete the given pattern as shown below.

16. *(a)* Option figure (a) will complete the given pattern as shown below.

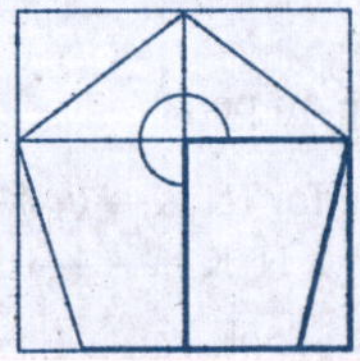

17. *(c)* The figure pattern in option (c) will complete the given pattern as shown below.

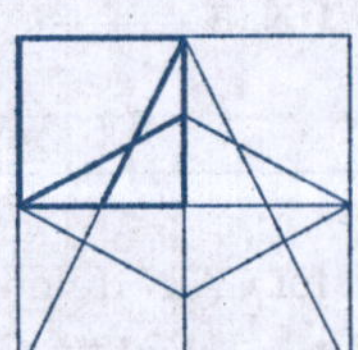

18. *(a)* The figure pattern in option (a) will complete the given pattern as shown below.

19. *(b)* The figure pattern in option (b) will complete the given pattern as shown below.

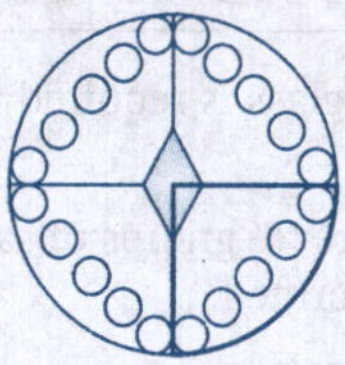

20. *(c)* The option figure (c) will complete the given pattern as shown below.

21. *(b)* Option figure (b) will complete the figure pattern as shown below.

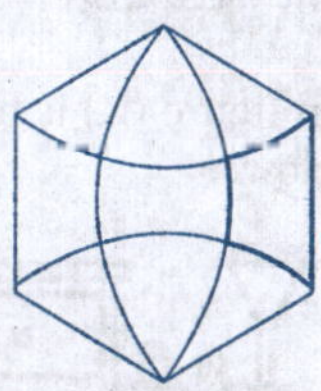

22. *(d)* The figure in option (d) will complete the given pattern as shown below.

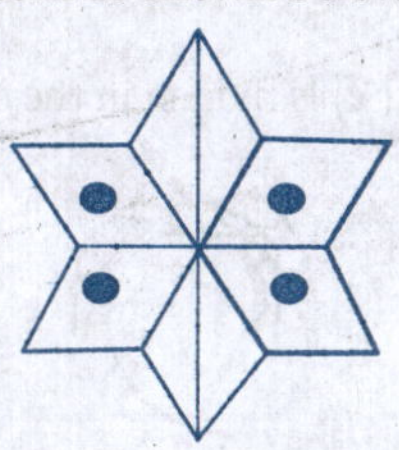

23. *(d)* The figure in option (d) will complete the given pattern as shown below.

24. *(b)* The figure in option (b) will complete the given pattern as shown below.

25. *(b)* The figure in option (b) will complete the given pattern as shown below.

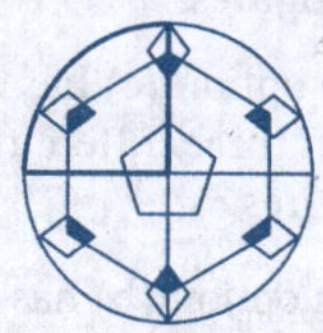

6. Find Similar Figure and Grouping of Figures

1. *(c)* Figure in option (c) has 5 lines as in the question figures.

2. *(c)* Figure in option (c) has opposite blocks shaded as in the question figures.

3. *(d)* Figure in option (d) has two opposite shapes in two parts as in the question figures.

4. *(a)* Figure in option (a) has one shaded and one unshaded circle at its ends as in the question figures.

5. *(c)* Figure in option (c) has two identical shapes overlapping at the bottom as in the question figures.

6. *(d)* Figure in option (d) has two squares on same line as in the question figures.

7. *(a)* Figure in option (a) has six blocks as in the question figures.

8. *(b)* Figure in option (b) has one circle, one triangle and one square as in the question figures.

9. *(c)* Figure in option (c) has a dotted shape inside the outer shape as in the question figures.

10. *(d)* Figure in option (d) is similar to the question figures having one dot at the bottom, two straight and one zig-zag lines.

11. *(c)* Figure in option (c) has one shaded and one unshaded shape (triangle) within a circle as in the question figures.

12. *(b)* Figure in option (b) has four 'T' shaped figures at its corners as in question figures.

13. *(a)* Figure in option (a) has two larger circles, one smaller circle and one shaded square as in question figures.

14. *(c)* Figure in option (c) has one, two and three dots on three different faces as in question figures.

15. *(b)* Figure in option (b) has 0, –, + and × symbols, as in question figures.

16. *(d)* Figure in option (d) is the mirror image as in the question figures.

17. *(c)* Figure in option (c) is inside the bigger shape of itself as in the question figures.

18. *(d)* Figure in option (d) has two stars and two circles as given in question figure.

19. *(c)* Figure in option (c) have two arrows in opposite direction as given in question figure.

20. *(d)* Figure in option (d) has three identical figures as given in question figures.

21. *(d)*

So, there are 6 groups of 2 teddy bears.

22. *(a)*

So, there are 4 stars in each group.

23. *(b)*

So, 1 more glass is required to form 4 groups of 4 glasses.

24. *(a)* There are '6' groups of same number of books are formed.

25. *(c)* There are '3' more caps are required to form 5 groups of 5 caps.

7. Hidden Figures

1. *(c)* The given figure is hidden in option figure (c) as shown below.

2. *(d)* The given figure (X) is hidden in train (d) as shown below.

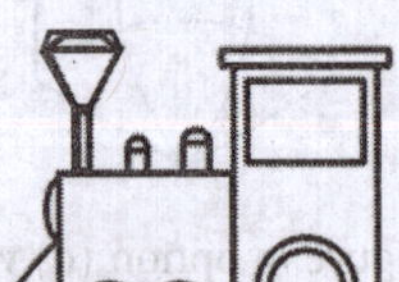

3. *(b)* Figure (X) is hidden in the option (b) mango.

4. *(a)* The given figure (X) is hidden in option figure (a) as shown below.

5. *(c)* The given shape (X) is hidden in option figure (c) as shown below.

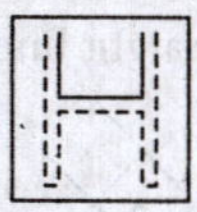

6. *(b)* The given figure (X) is hidden in option figure (b) as shown below.

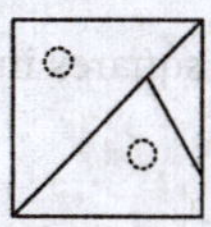

7. *(b)* The given figure (X) is hidden in option figure (b) as shown below.

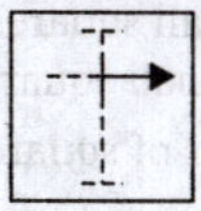

8. *(c)* The given figure (X) is hidden in option figure (c) as shown below.

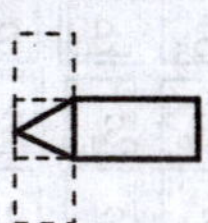

9. *(c)* Figure (X) is hidden in the option (c).

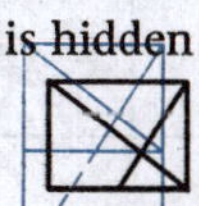

10. *(a)* Figure (X) is hidden in the given figure of option (a).

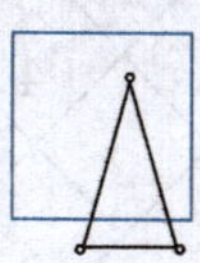

11. *(d)* Figure (X) is hidden in the option figure (d).

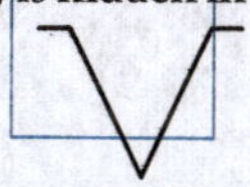

12. *(c)* Figure (X) is hidden in the option figure (c).

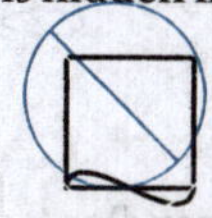

13. *(c)* Figure (X) is hidden in the option figure (c).

14. *(d)* The part given in option figure (d) is hidden in the given figure (X) as shown below.

15. *(b)* The part given in option (b) is hidden in the given figure (X) as shown below.

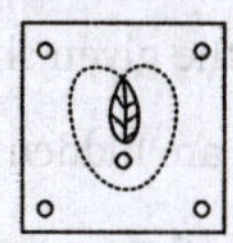

16. *(c)* Shape given in option (c) is hidden in the given figure (X) as shown below.

17. *(d)* The part given in option figure (d) is hidden in the given figure (X) as shown below

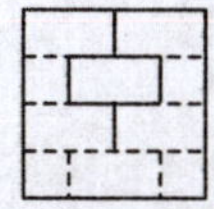

18. *(a)* Shape given in option figure (a) is hidden in figure (X) as shown below

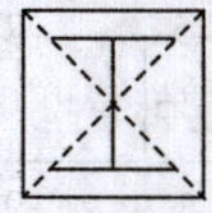

19. *(d)* Figure given in option (d) is hidden in the given figure (X) as shown below

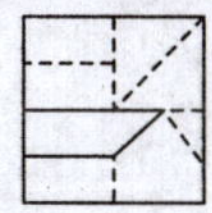

20. (a) Option (a) figure '' is hidden in the given figure (X).

21. (c) The hidden candles '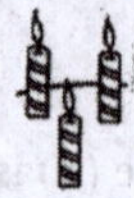' is given in the option (c).

22. (b) The given part '' is hidden in the group (b).

23. *(b)* Shape given in option (b) is hidden in the given figure.

24. *(a)* Two pictures, i.e.  and  are hidden in the given figure.

25. *(d)* Option (d) shape is hidden in part (3) of the picture.

26. *(a)* In part '1' the given shape is hidden.

27. *(d)* '4' pictures are hidden in the given picture.

8. Counting of Figures

1. *(b)*

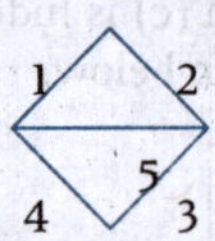

So, there are 5 straight lines in the given figure.

2. *(d)*

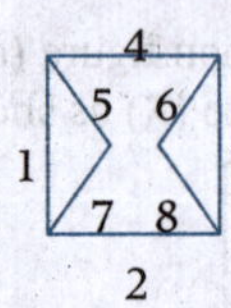

So, there are 8 straight lines in the given figure.

3. *(d)*

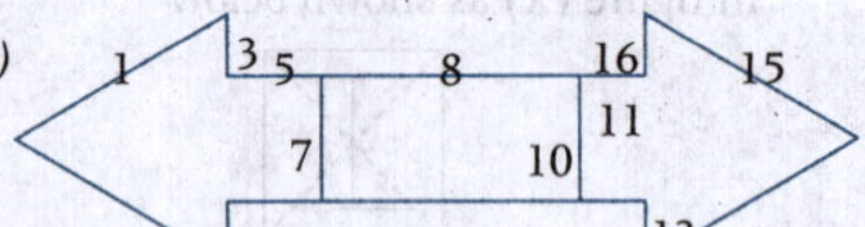

There are 16 straight lines in the figure.

4. *(c)*

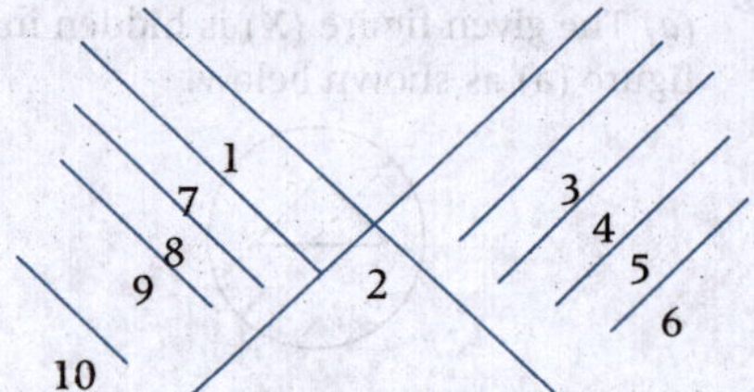

There are 10 straight lines.

5. *(c)*

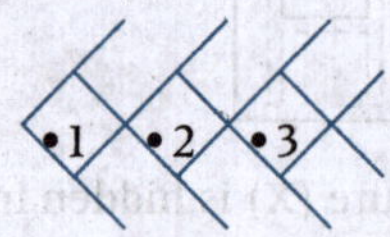

So, there are 3 squares in the given figure.

6. *(a)*

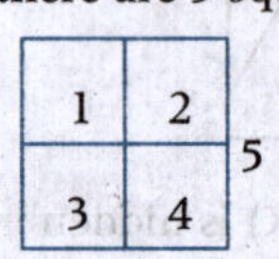

There are 4 small squares and 1 large square containing 4 small squares.

∴ Total number of squares = 4 + 1 = 5

7. *(c)*

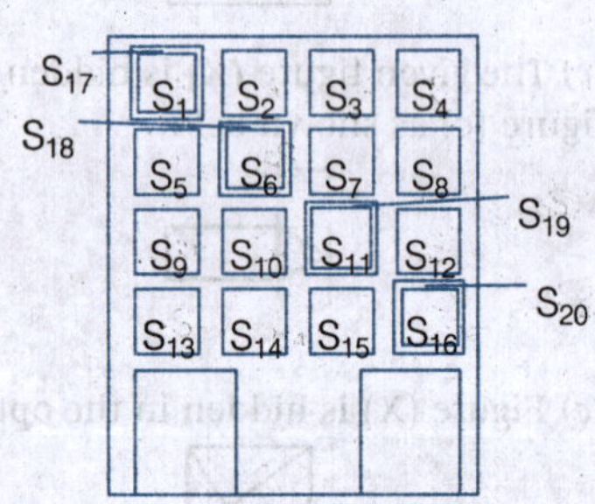

So, there are 20 squares in the given figure.

8. *(d)* Only figure (d) contains exactly four squares.

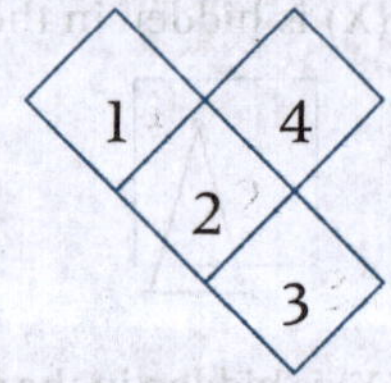

9. *(c)*

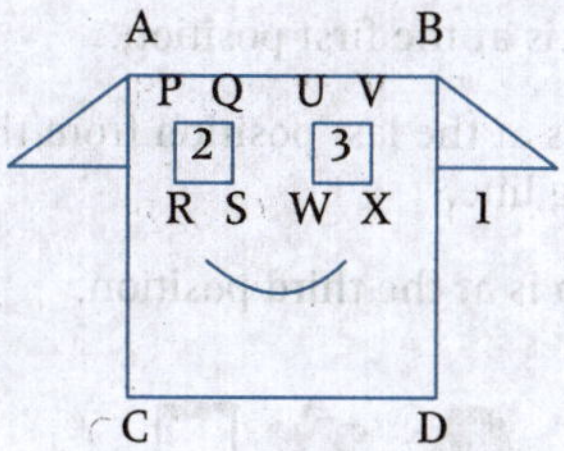

There are three squares

1 large square + 2 small squares.

10. *(c)*

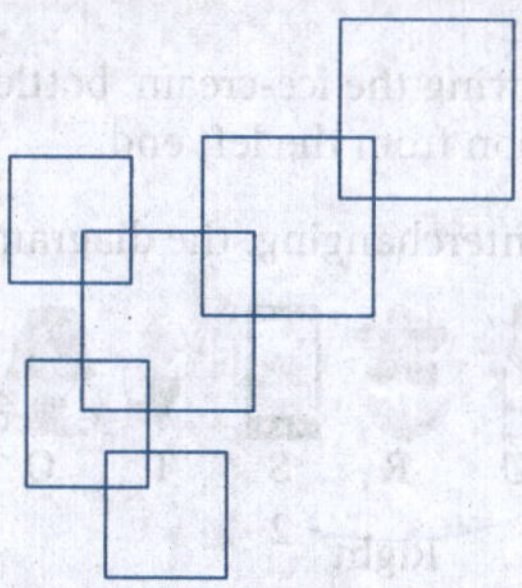

There are 6 squares present in the figure.

11. *(d)*

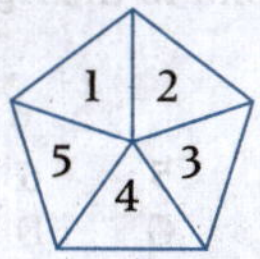

So, there are 5 triangles in the given figure.

12. *(a)*

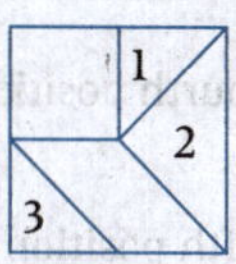

So, there are 3 triangles in the given figure.

13. *(b)* There are '6' triangles present in the figure.

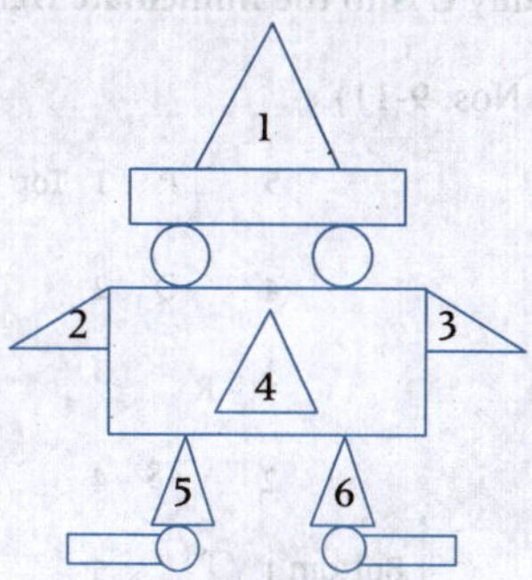

14. *(b)*

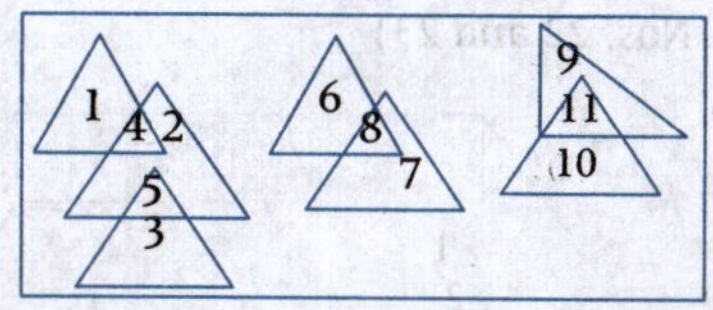

There are '11' triangles are present in the figure.

15. *(a)*

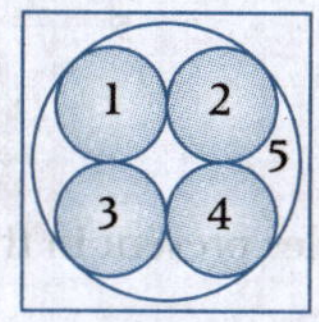

So, there are 5 circles in the given figure.

16. *(d)*

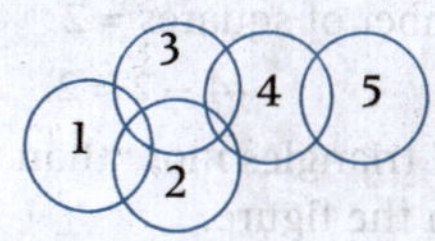

So, there are 5 circles in given figure.

17. *(b)*

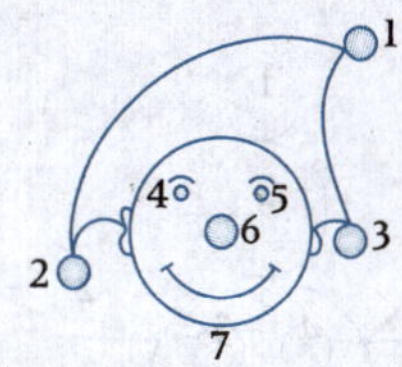

So, there are 7 circles in the given figure.

18. *(b)* There are '8' circles present in the given figure.

19. *(a)* 4 shapes i.e. P, Q, S and T have triangular shapes.

20. *(d)*

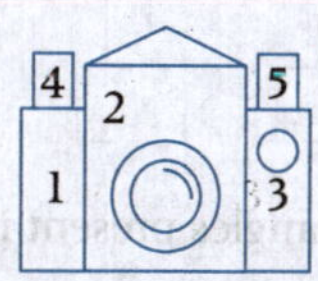

So, there are 5 rectangles in the given figure.

21. *(a)*

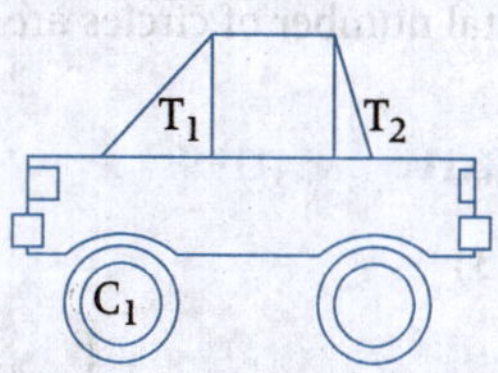

So, there are 2 triangles and 4 circles in the given figure.

Sol. (Q. Nos. 22 and 23)

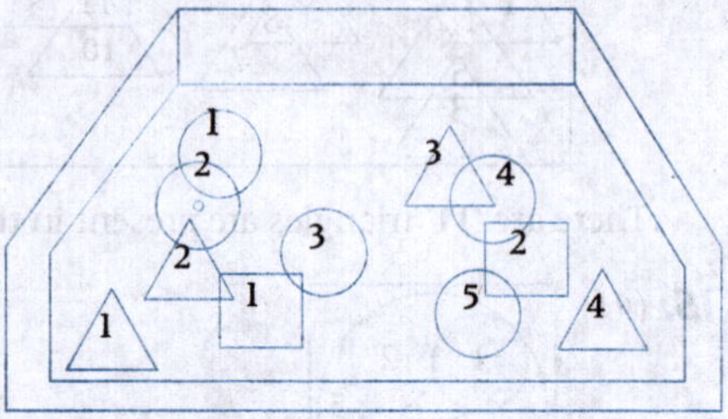

22. *(d)* There are '5' circles present in the given figure.

23. *(a)* Total number of triangles = 4

Total number of squares = 2

So, 4 − 2 = 2

Hence, '2' triangles more than squares are present in the figure.

Sol. (Q. Nos. 24 and 25)

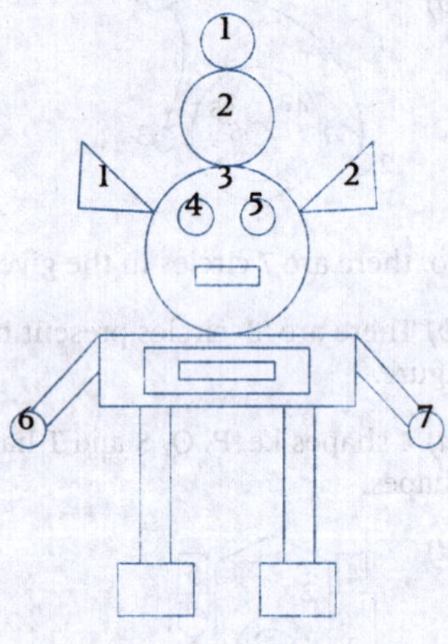

24. *(b)* There are '2' triangles present in the figure.

25. *(c)* The total number of circles are '7'.

9. Position and Comparison Test

Sol. (Q. Nos. 1-3)

5 (last)	4	3	2	1	FINISH (Right)
Joy	Tim	Flora	Brane	Paul	

1. *(d)* Paul is at the first position.

2. *(a)* Joy is at the last position from the finishing line.

3. *(b)* Flora is at the third position.

4. *(d)*

P	Q	R	S		U	V
1	2	3	4		5	6
Left						Right

After removing the ice-cream, bottle is at the fifth position from the left end.

5. *(a)* After interchanging, the diagram will be

P	U	R	S	T	Q	V
Left	Right		2			Right

After interchanging the positions, element 'S' i.e. phone will be second to the right of bottle.

Sol. (Q. Nos. 6-8)

→ Start Left	1	2	3	4	5	6	7	← Last Right
	B	E	A	C	G	D	F	
	7	6	5	4	3	2	1	

6. *(a)* Teddy C is at the fourth position from the start.

7. *(c)* Teddy A is at the fifth position from the last.

8. *(b)* Teddy A is at the third position and teddy C is to the immediate right of teddy A.

Sol. (Q. Nos. 9-11)

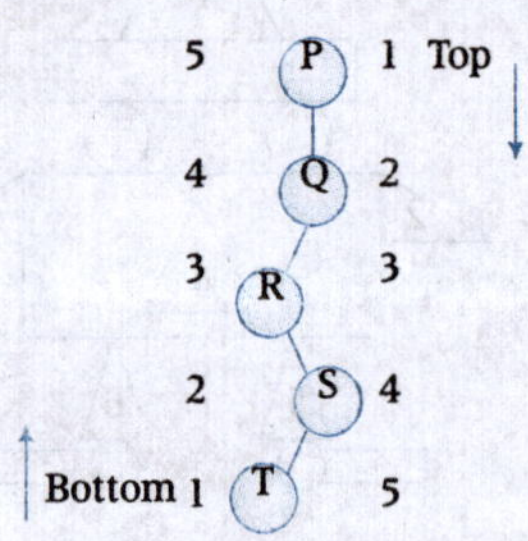

9. (b) Bead Q is fourth from the bottom.

10. (c) Bead R is at the middle position.

11. (b) Bead T is at the fifth position from the top.

Sol. (Q. Nos. 12 and 13)

Left ⟶
Ride Ray John Julia Marie Jack Lina
⟵ Right

12. (c) Ray is sixth from the right.

13. (b) John is third from the left.

14. (c) Pilot M1 is third to the left of pilot X1.

15. (b) Pilot 'U1' is fourth to the right of first pilot from the left.

16. (d) Pilot 'X1' is third from the right end.

17. (b) Cat 'C2' is third to the left of rat R4.

18. (b) Cat 'C1' is third from the right end after interchanged their positions.

19. (b) If we remove all the rats, then cat 'C2' is immediate left of cat 'C3'.

20. (c) 'P3' is sixth from the left end.

21. (d) 'P4' will be third from the left of boy 'P3' after interchange the positions.

22. (a) 'Hat N' is fifth from the top.

23. (b) There are two hats between 'Hat O' and 'Hat P'.

24. (c) Ciki is in middle of the arrangement.

25. (a) Orange is sixth from the right end.

26. (b) Fourth to the left of third letter from the right end will be 7th letter from the right end i.e., Q.

27. (c) The number third from the right is 112.
The number third from the left is 98.
Difference $= 112 - 98 = 14$

28. (a) Star with number '38' is middle of the arrangement.

29. (d) After interchanging, the diagram will be

Left ⟶

P Q U S T R V W

⟵ Right

After interchanging, U will be sixth from the right.

30. (c) 5th, 6th, 7th, 8th, 9th, 10th, 11th, 12th
There are 6 stairs between 5th stair and 12th stair.

Practice Set 1

1. (b) Each figure repeats itself after every three figures. So, the next figure will be .

2. (d) Except figure (d), all others are divided into three parts. But figure (d) is divided into four parts. So, option figure (d) does not fit into the group.

3. (c) The figure in option (c) will complete the pattern as shown below.

4. (d) The number of elements becomes six from one in second figure. So, the figure in option (d) will complete the second pair.

5. (d) Except (d), all others are stationery items. So, figure (d) is different from others.

6. (a) The pattern is as follows

$$18 \xrightarrow{+4} 22 \xrightarrow{+4} 26 \xrightarrow{+4} 30 \xrightarrow{+4} \boxed{34}$$

So, 34 will come next in the given series.

7. (c) In first pair, the shaded circle is covered by a circle.
Similarly, in second pair, the shaded square will be covered by a square. So, figure in option (c) will complete the second pair.

8. *(b)* As, $7 \times 5 = 35$

Similarly, $9 \times 6 = \boxed{54}$

So, 54 is the missing number.

9. *(c)* 4 groups of 4 candies can be formed from the given candies as shown below.

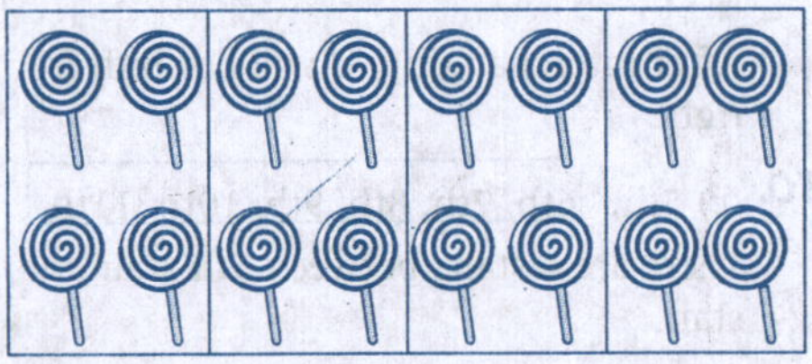

1 2 3 4

10. *(c)* Shape given in option (c) has 3 shaded sides as given group of shapes.

11. *(b)* Option figure (b) is hidden in the given figure (X) as shown below.

12. *(a)* The colour of milk is White but here White is called Pink. So, the colour of milk is Pink.

13. *(c)* The circles can be counted as

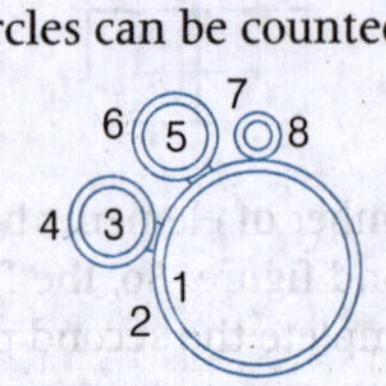

So, there are 8 circles in the given figure.

14. *(a)* Monkey 'K' is sixth from the right end.

15. *(d)* As, 9 7 0 ⟶ 0 7 9

Similarly, 8 1 6 ⟶ $\boxed{6\ 1\ 8}$

16. *(c)* As, $P \rightarrow 16 - 1 = 15$

$M \rightarrow 13 - 1 = 12$

$J \rightarrow 10 - 1 = 9$

$C \rightarrow 3 - 1 = 2$

Similarly, C ⟶ 3–1 = $\boxed{2}$

Q ⟶ 17–1 = $\boxed{16}$

X ⟶ 24–1 = $\boxed{23}$

I ⟶ 9–1 = $\boxed{8}$

17. *(c)* As, R $\xrightarrow{+3}$ U $\xrightarrow{+3}$ X

J $\xrightarrow{+3}$ M $\xrightarrow{+3}$ P

C $\xrightarrow{+3}$ F $\xrightarrow{+4}$ $\boxed{J}$

X $\xrightarrow{+3}$ A $\xrightarrow{+3}$ D

Hene, option (c) is odd.

18. *(b)* The pattern is as follows

D $\xrightarrow{+4}$ H $\xrightarrow{+2}$ J $\xrightarrow{+4}$ N $\xrightarrow{+2}$ P $\xrightarrow{+4}$ T $\xrightarrow{+2}$ $\boxed{V}$ $\xrightarrow{+4}$ $\boxed{Z}$

Hence, missing pair of letters are VZ.

19. *(a)* As, S I G N A L

I S N G L A

Similarly, S U M M E R

$\boxed{\text{U S M M R E}}$

20. *(d)* The pattern is as follows

J① — K② — L③ — M④ — N⑤ — O⑥

21. *(b)* As, the sum of all digits in numbers here are '13' while the sum of digits in '7133' is

$7 + 1 + 3 + 3 = 14$.

22. *(b)* The pattern is completed by the option (b).

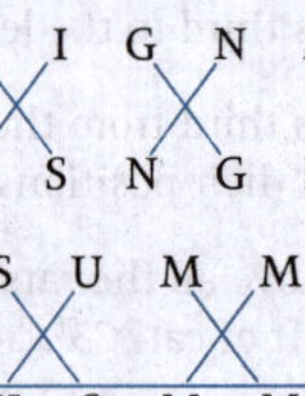

23. *(c)* As, we know that the colour of 'Mango' is 'Yellow' and here 'Yellow' is called 'Apple'.

24. *(b)* The option (b) shape is belongs to the given group of shapes.
i.e. 

25. *(a)* The option(a) shape is hidden in the given picture.

26. *(c)* There are '9' circles present in the given figure.

27. *(c)* The shape in option (c) is belongs to the group of shapes given.

28. *(c)* There are '6' triangles in the pattern.

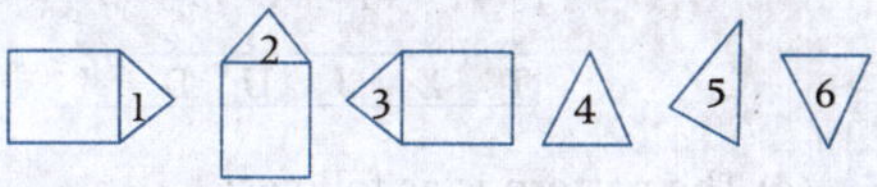

29. *(b)* In part '2' the shape is hidden.

30. *(b)* The shape in option (b) is hidden in part 3.

31. *(c)* If 'Car C' and 'Car A' interchange their positions, then 'Car C' is third from the left end.

32. *(a)* We need '12' trees to form the '6' groups of 2 trees. Here we have only '11'. So, we need 1 more tree.

33. *(b)* Option (b) figure contains exactly three squares.

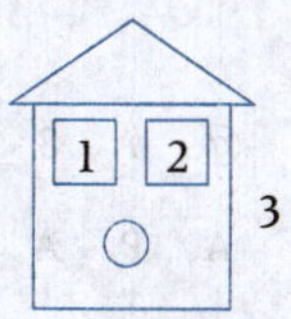

34. *(d)* When we removed the 'Kite', then 'Tree' is second to the left of third object from the right end.

35. *(b)* The pattern is as follows

4 —×3→ 12 —×3→ 36 —×3→ 108 —×3→ 324 —×3→ [972]

So, the missing term is 972.

Practice Set 2

1. *(b)* As, C A T ⟶ T A C

Similarly, R A T ⟶ T A R

2. *(d)* Figure in option (d) will complete the given figure (X) as shown below

3. *(b)* All the flowers have five petals except flower in option (b). So, opiton (b) is odd one out.

4. *(a)* From first to second figure a star appears within the given shape. So, option figure (a) will complete the second pair.

5. *(c)* Each figure repeats itself after every three figures. So, the missing figure will be 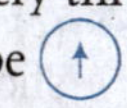.

6. *(b)* Barber cuts our hair but here barber is called postman. So, postman cuts our hair.

7. *(c)* Figure (c) has two similar shapes as given in question figures.

8. *(a)* Gloves are worn in hands while all others are worn in foot. So, figure (a) is different from others.

9. *(b)* The pattern is as follows

$1 \xrightarrow{+3} 4 \xrightarrow{+3} 7 \xrightarrow{+3} \boxed{10}$

So, there will be 10 caps in pattern 4.

10. *(a)* After removing the star the arrangement will be

So, the sixth item will be

11. *(b)* The pattern is as follows

25 31 37 43 49 (55)

+6 +6 +6 +6 +6

So, the missing number will be 55.

12. *(a)*

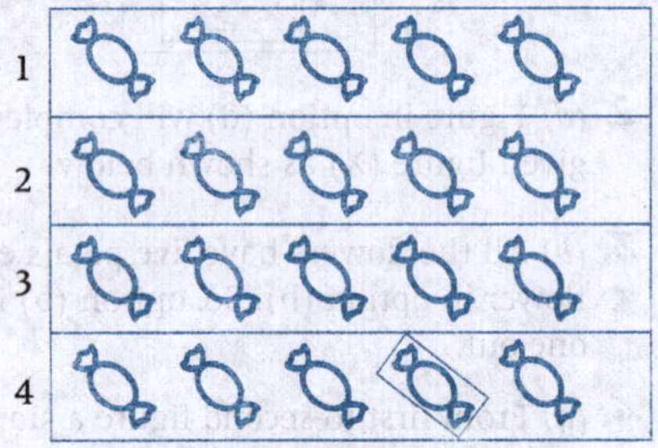

Thus, one toffee is required to form 4 groups of 5 toffees.

13. *(c)* There are 9 squares in the given figure as shown below

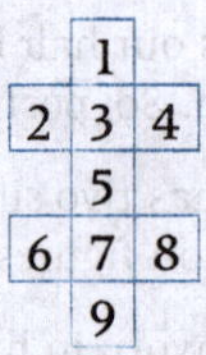

14. *(d)* The number represents the number of straight lines in the given shape. Thus, the shape in second pair has 4 number of lines.

15. *(b)* Shape in option (b) is hidden in the given figure (X) as shown below

16. *(b)* As,

D M J P

+3 +3 +3 +3

G P M S

Similarly,

Z X B N

+3 +3 +3 +3

C A E Q

17. *(c)* Except option (c) all are multiple of '7'.

18. *(a)* As, in first row we have given table of 8 up to '4'.

Similarly, in second row we have given table of '5' upto 4.

So, $5 \times 3 = 15$

19. *(c)* As,

P A Y A L

+1 +1 +1 +1 +1

Q B Z B M

Similarly,

S W I T C H

+1 +1 +1 +1 +1 +1

T X J U D I

20. *(a)* The pattern is as follows:

$M_1NO_2PQR_3STUV_4WXYZA_5$

21. *(d)* As, $7+1=8$, $9+5=14$, $6+2=8$

$3+1=4 \neq 8$

So, '318' is odd number.

22. *(d)* Option figure (d) complete the figure (X).

23. *(b)* As,

S I Y A

1 @ # 8

and

P A P A

3 8 3 8

Similarly,

P I Y A

3 @ # 8

24. *(c)* In both P, Q groups shape  is hidden.

25. *(b)* The given picture is hidden in the part 3.

26. *(d)* There are '5' triangles in the given figure.

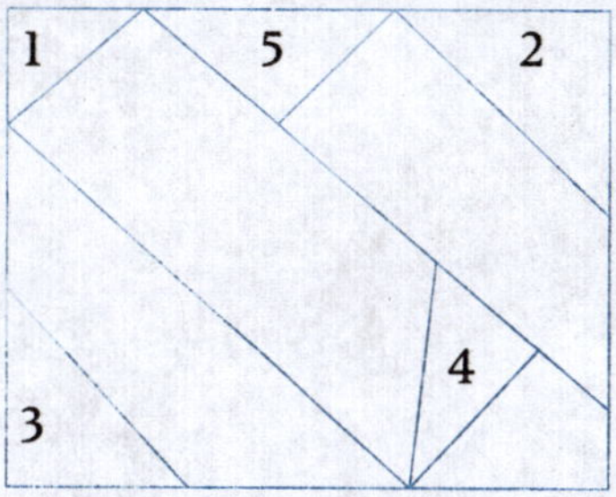

27. *(a)* Option (a) shape belongs to the group of shapes.

28. *(a)* The option (a) shape is hidden in part '3'.

29. *(a)* The given picture is hidden in part '1'.

30. *(c)* There are '8' circles present in the given shape.

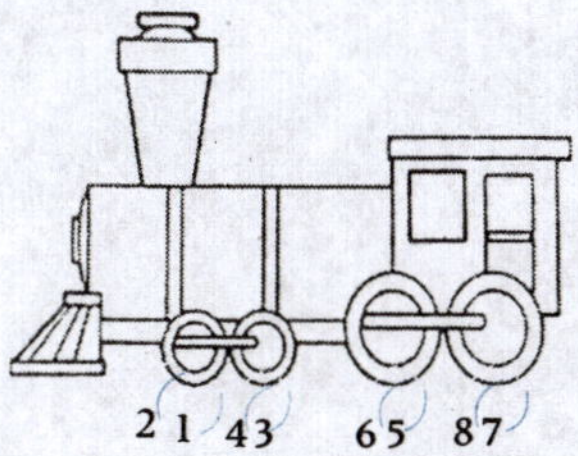

31. *(a)* 'E1' is 5th from the right end.

32. *(b)* We have 15 bowls here. So, '5' bowls are there in each group if '3' groups of equal number of bowls are formed.

33. *(b)* There are '4' triangles and '6' squares are present in the given figure.

34. *(b)* The pattern is as follows :

$181 \xrightarrow{+5} 186 \xrightarrow{+5} 191 \xrightarrow{+5} 196 \xrightarrow{+5} \boxed{201}$

The missing number is 201.

35. *(c)* Kid which is third to the left of the third kid from the end is 6th kid from the right end i.e., Zack.